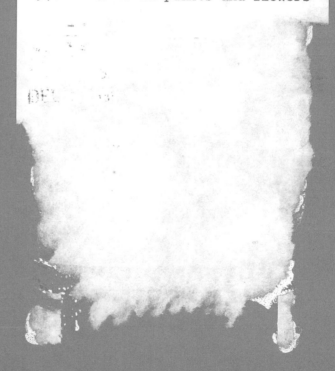

Color in
Plants
and
Flowers

JOHN AND SUSAN PROCTOR

Color in
Plants
and
Flowers

Foreword by Professor Alan Gemmell

Everest House
Publishers   *New York*

The deep purple of clematis petals is caused by pigments dissolved in the cell sap. Against the strong background colour, the flower's fertile parts stand out clearly to attract insect pollinators.

Library of Congress Catalog Card No. 78–56356
ISBN 0–89696–017–X

Copyright © 1978 by Eurobook Limited

Published simultaneously in
Canada by Beaverbooks, Pickering, Ontario

Printed in England by William Clowes, Beccles

Contents

Variegated leaf of a garden pelargonium.
Some types of leaf variegation can be
inherited by the seed. Others are caused by
various diseases and can only be
maintained from cuttings.

Foreword

A good book on plants and their colours has been very long overdue for the subject is vast, complex, and the information has to be gleaned from many and varied sources. At last here is such a book which collects a great mass of unusual and fascinating information, digests it, simplifies it and then presents it to the reader in an interesting and absorbing manner.

To me this book has many assets for it combines scientific accuracy with a degree of simplification in such a way that points are made and not lost, and the absolute novice in the scientific world can follow the most difficult passages with not too much effort. The science of plant colours is complicated and many aspects of it are as yet unexplained, but if science is to be made intelligible to the layman then this is the way to do it.

Three groups of people will find this book a treasure of unusual, useful and interesting material. Firstly it will appeal to all gardeners who have looked at their plants and wondered about red cabbage, golden daffodils, striped tulips, variegated ivy, and all the kaleidoscope of flower colours which the garden shows all the year round. What use are these colours? How did they arise? What caused them in the first place? All sorts of questions spring to mind whenever gardens and flowers are mentioned, and here are many answers and some thought-provoking suggestions.

The second group is the vast number of naturalists and those interested in ecology who see in their travels and in the wild places of this country the complex interplay of insect and plant, of animals and their food, and who discern in the colours around them a scientific challenge and a whole language waiting to be interpreted. Here is a combination of beauty and biology full of interest and strangely fascinating.

The third group includes the student, the scientifically curious layman and all who would welcome the chance offered in this book to approach a new type of biology where the laboratory and the wilderness meet. Here they will find scientific accuracy, careful writing and challenging ideas. There is here a blend of the academic and the practical which is a pleasure to read.

And to all who just want a really good book to read I recommend this as being full of stimulating ideas and even of scientific detective work.

Alan Gemmell

Introduction

For most of the time that human beings have been on Earth their surroundings have been dominated by plant colours. Only in places which man, too, finds inhospitable, are plant colours inconspicuous. The polar regions are white from ice and snow, the deserts a combination of yellows, reds and greys from the exposed rocks. Elsewhere the greens of living plants predominate, interrupted in areas where there are marked seasonal effects with the browns of dead leaves and stems.

Nowadays, however, the position is changing rapidly. An increasing proportion of mankind is permanently in towns and cities, and concrete and tarmacadam have replaced plants as the background against which we live.

The spurred orange flowers of *Tropaeolum* are coloured by a combination of red cell sap and yellow pigments in the cell protoplasm.

One of the first surprising things about plant colours is that our range of vision coincides with them. The coincidence is not perfect for plants do produce colours that we cannot see, but nevertheless it is fairly closely matched. The answer lies in the properties of light of different wavelengths. Light of longer wavelengths than red is too low in energy for most plants to harness or for warm-blooded animals to perceive sensitively. Light of much shorter wavelengths than violet is too violently disruptive and cannot be tolerated by either plants or animals. Fortunately only a little of this short wavelength light reaches the earth's surface nowadays and biologically detectable and usable light is therefore confined to a fairly narrow range of wavelengths, most of which are within our range of vision.

Plants are overwhelmingly green and this is of prime importance. The green plant pigment chlorophyll is a vital substance; it captures sunlight and enables plants both to feed all life on earth and to provide oxygen for breathing. Many of the other plant colours in nature are concerned with summoning animals for the plants' pollination and fruit and seed dispersal, which ensures the survival of the species.

There are also plant colours which are much more mysterious, even apparently inexplicable. Some of these seemingly functionless colours, such as the many autumnal colours in trees, can perhaps be interpreted as accidentally colourful waste disposal by the plants. In some cases the plant actually appears to handicap itself by being colourful, as for example in the deep purple spotted leaves of common British orchids of the genus *Dactylorhiza*. The dark spots seem to mask part of the leaf and make it less effective at using sunlight, yet the orchids thrive, growing well together with non-spotted relatives. There are a number of instances where the development of a colour is so involved that although it seems useless, we intuitively suspect there must be some useful reason for its existence. The finest examples are the cases of light production in plants, involving complicated chemistry but having no clear function.

It is appropriate to end this introduction by acknowledging our debt to plants for enabling us to see their colours at all. Animal vision depends on substances called carotenoids which no animal is able to manufacture on its own. Instead, animals rely entirely on the carotenoids made by plants, obtaining them when they eat either the plants themselves or other, herbivorous animals. Plants, therefore not only support our own and all animals' existence with their chlorophyll; they also provide key substances for vision and enable us to delight in their colours.

Yet for many of us, who perhaps are not fully adjusted to the enormity of changes that urbanization has imposed, plant colours are essential. This need is recognized by town planners and terms like 'green belt' reflect our efforts to preserve plant colours. Gardens of sizes from a single plant pot to several square kilometres provide a source of relaxation and pleasure to townspeople and country landowners alike. Gardening is the most popular hobby in the western world and provides us with a whole range of vivid plant colours. Man has selected and bred ornamental plants for thousands of years and in his enthusiasm has often given gardens a mass of colours unparalleled in natural vegetation.

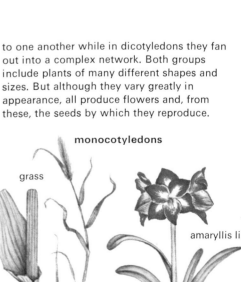

brown algae   club mosses   ferns   monocots   dicots

flowering plants

Plant evolution

Plants evolved in the sea around 3,000 million years ago and about 400 million years ago the first land plants appeared. Gradually, many different groups evolved. Some, such as the seed ferns, became extinct but other ancient plants such as horsetails, ferns and club mosses have survived. Today, by far the most important land plants are the flowering plants, which now include around 250,000 species.

What is a plant?

Plants which together with animals make up the two great kingdoms of the living world, are more easily recognized than defined. The larger types have certain obvious characteristics in common: they consist of roots fixed in the soil and an aerial shoot, the stem, on which green leaves usually grow. The flowering plants, probably the most familiar group of all to most people, produce flowers at certain times of the year from which fruits and seeds develop. However, plants are immensely variable, ranging from tiny algae to giant conifers. While the larger may be easily grouped, the very smallest organisms are so difficult to define that some have been classified as both plants and animals.

In general, plants differ from animals because they are stationary and use light energy to manufacture their food instead of relying on other plants and animals. Even here there are exceptions: many algae are mobile at some stage of their life cycle and though only plants can harness the energy of sunlight, not all do so. The eleven groups shown on the evolutionary diagram are now accepted as true plants. Of these the flowering plants, the latest group to evolve, now dominate the world's vegetation.

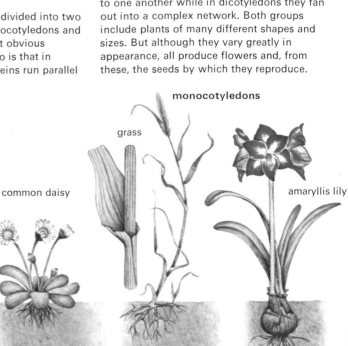

Flowering plants

Left: Flowering plants are divided into two main sub-groups, the monocotyledons and the dicotyledons. The most obvious difference between the two is that in monocotyledons the leaf veins run parallel to one another while in dicotyledons they fan out into a complex network. Both groups include plants of many different shapes and sizes. But although they vary greatly in appearance, all produce flowers and, from these, the seeds by which they reproduce.

dicotyledons

elm   cabbage   common daisy

monocotyledons

grass   amaryllis lily

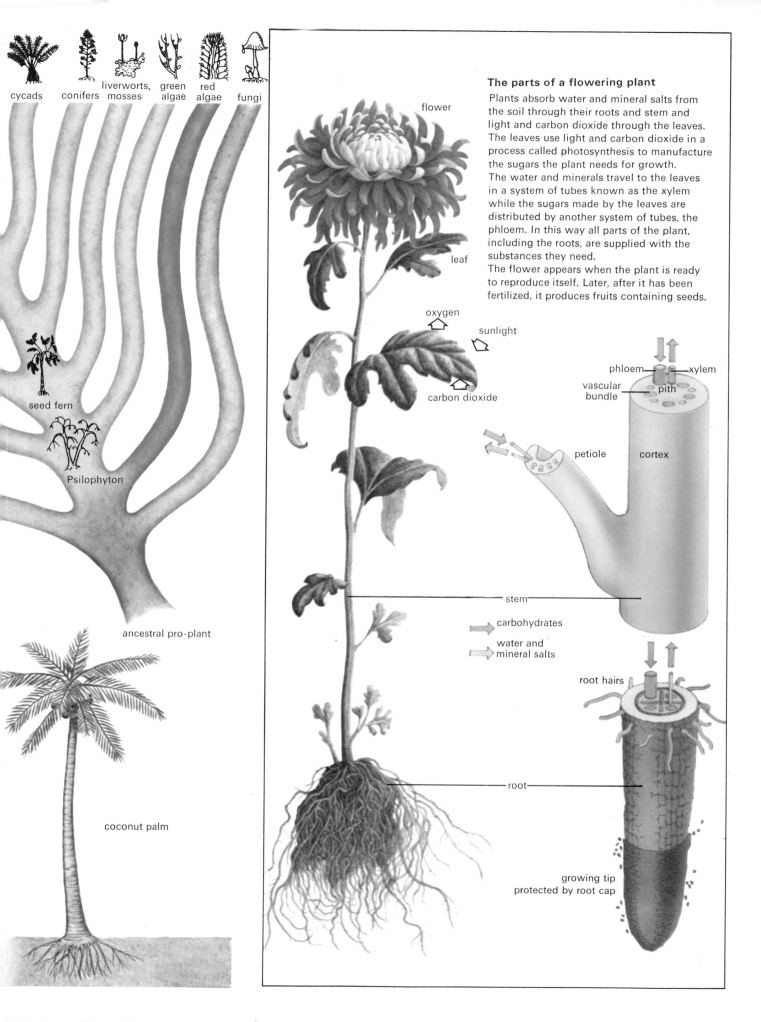

cycads

conifers

liverworts, mosses

green algae

red algae

fungi

seed fern

Psilophyton

ancestral pro-plant

coconut palm

flower

leaf

oxygen

sunlight

carbon dioxide

The parts of a flowering plant

Plants absorb water and mineral salts from the soil through their roots and stem and light and carbon dioxide through the leaves. The leaves use light and carbon dioxide in a process called photosynthesis to manufacture the sugars the plant needs for growth.

The water and minerals travel to the leaves in a system of tubes known as the xylem while the sugars made by the leaves are distributed by another system of tubes, the phloem. In this way all parts of the plant, including the roots, are supplied with the substances they need.

The flower appears when the plant is ready to reproduce itself. Later, after it has been fertilized, it produces fruits containing seeds.

phloem

xylem

vascular bundle

pith

petiole

cortex

stem

carbohydrates

water and mineral salts

root hairs

root

growing tip protected by root cap

How plant colours are made

The nature of light and colour

The colours of everything we see around us are all part of the effect of light. Nearly all our light comes to us from the sun and before it reaches the Earth has travelled through tens of millions of kilometres of space. If the light is not blocked or reflected in any way it travels in straight lines. According to one theory all light consists of a stream of small particles called photons or quanta, but many facts about light cannot be explained in this way. In some of its manifestations light behaves rather like waves on water and it is then interpreted not as particles but as a wave moving along. The question of whether light is waves or particles has never been resolved and which theory is used depends on the phenomenon that is being explained. At the present stage of human knowledge no single theory adequately covers all aspects of light.

The different colours which make up light can be explained using the wave theory because of the existence of different wavelengths. Light of wavelengths from 0.00038mm to 0.0005mm appears violet to blue-green; from 0.0005mm to 0.0006mm appears green to yellow and from 0.0006mm to 0.00075mm appears orange to red. Light of wavelengths shorter than 0.00038mm is called ultra-violet, that greater than 0.00075mm is called infra-red. Both ultra-violet and infra-red light are invisible to humans but are of great importance to all living things.

Light comes from the sun in a mixture of different wavelengths. The mixture is split into its components naturally in rainbows and was first split experimentally into the colours of the spectrum about three hundred years ago by the famous scientist Sir Isaac Newton. He used a prism to separate out the range of colours of

Fall colours of maples, elms and birches with evergreen conifers, in New England. Though the leaves of deciduous trees die every year, the splendour of their colour change cannot be predicted with certainty. The development of orange and yellow carotenoids and anthocyanin pigments depends on the weather. Their colours show as the dominant green chlorophyll pigments degenerate with age. The best autumn colours develop after a warm summer, followed by low but not freezing temperatures.

In very dim light we see no colours. The cells in our eyes which give us vision in these conditions are called rods and we cannot perceive colours with them. The cells which give us colour vision, the cones, function only in brighter light.

Rainbows are caused by tiny water droplets in the atmosphere reflecting and refracting sunlight and splitting it into its component colours. We can see the colours only at a particular distance and angle and this is why rainbows are usually arc-shaped.

visible light: violet, blue, blue-green, green, yellow, orange and red – the colours of the rainbow. Colour is also produced when the mixture of wavelengths falls on a substance which absorbs and reflects some light wavelengths more than others, and it is this that causes most plant colours.

The substances which upset the balance of spectral colours in this way are called pigments. Blue pigment looks blue because it absorbs all colours except blue, which it reflects or transmits. A black pigment looks black because it absorbs light of all colours. Pigments do not have a colour themselves, but it is customary to refer to them as being blue, red, green and so on.

Describing plant colours

As soon as we start looking closely at plants we notice that the colours we observe are never exactly the same. Red flowers, green leaves all differ in their precise colour between plants or even on the same plant. Scientists have solved the problem of defining colour exactly by having a set of standard colours of which the 'Munsell Color Charts' are the most widely used. In these charts colours

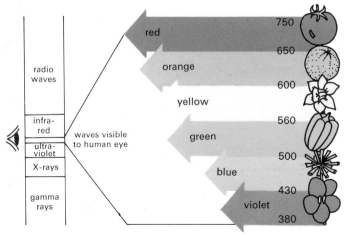

sunlight

The waves here are measured in nanometres. A nanometre is one millionth of a millimetre.

Light is part of a continuous spectrum of electromagnetic radiation from the sun. All radiations in the spectrum travel in waves, varying in length from those of gamma and X-rays, measured in hundredths of millionths of a millimetre, to those of low frequency radio waves, measured in kilometres. The longest light wavelength visible to man is red, the shortest is violet. When light comes from the sun it is a mixture of different wavelengths and looks colourless. Colour is caused when the light falls on a substance such as a pigment in a plant cell which absorbs and reflects some wavelengths more than others.

are described by three attributes, hue, value and chroma. Whole ranges of charts with various combinations of these are used for accurate scientific comparisons.

The hues are the five principal classes of plant colours, red, yellow, green, blue and purple. These are sub-divided into intermediate hue names of yellow-red, green-yellow etc, then further split into ten steps each. There is a hue range of a hundred units.

The value of a colour describes its degree of lightness or darkness, while the chroma shows its strength or saturation. The complete Munsell notation for any colour is written with numerical values for hue, value/chroma. For example a dark green might be 2.5G 4/6. These notations will not be used to describe colours in this book but they do highlight the difficulties of being precise about a particular colour.

How plants produce colours

The means by which nature produces plant colours are basically fairly simple. Relatively few pigment types are used although, as we shall see later, there is an additional physical way by which white and other effects are produced without pigments.

Plants are composed of microscopic boxes called cells, each with its own controlling nucleus. The inside of the cell is called the vacuole and contains the cell sap. This is enclosed by a membrane and surrounded by a layer of protoplasm, the basic living matter of the plant. A cell wall, normally composed of a type of cellulose, divides each cell from those around it.

The chemical pigments which give a plant colour usually belong to one of three groups, each group occurring in a different part of the cell. Those that occur in the cell vacuoles, dissolved in cell sap, are known as vacuolar pigments. These include two important types known as anthoxanthins and anthocyanins, which provide a great variety of different colours. The second group, which are insoluble in water but soluble in fats, sometimes occur in oil droplets within the cell but more often in special structures called plastids found in the protoplasm of the cells. Plastid pigments include the chlorophylls (all green) and carotenoids (various orange, red and brownish colours). The final group, involving a large number of substances to which no simple class can be given, are found in the walls of the cells.

The characteristic and most important colour of plants is green. Although there is an enormous variety of greens they are all, with a few exceptions, produced in the same way, through the pigment chlorophyll. Chlorophyll is contained within small green plastids called chloroplasts which in most land plants are small, convex-lens shaped

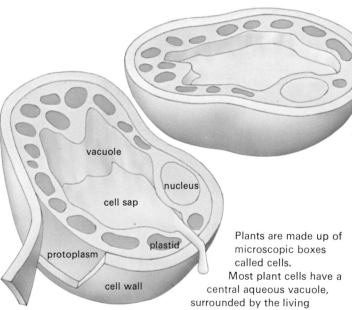

Plants are made up of microscopic boxes called cells.

Most plant cells have a central aqueous vacuole, surrounded by the living protoplasm which contains the nucleus. The pigments which give a plant its colour are produced by the cells and deposited in three main sites within them.

Cell walls are coloured by a wide variety of pigments (black, brown, yellow, red, blue and violet) which may often make the cell completely opaque.

The protoplasm is coloured by fat-soluble pigments carried in special structures called plastids. Plastid pigments include chlorophyll (green) and carotenoids (yellow, orange, red and brown).

The cell sap is coloured by water-soluble vacuolar pigments. These include anthocyanins (scarlet through magenta and purple to blue) and anthoxanthins (pale ivory to deep yellow)

Left: Plants living in harsh, waterless desert environments must be specially adapted. The leaves of cacti are reduced to spines to cut down evaporation from their surface. They also store water in their swollen stems. In the organpipe cacti shown here, the process of photosynthesis takes place largely in the green, outer cells of the stems.

Right: Silversword growing on Mt Haleakala, Hawaii. Its glaucous leaves are clothed in silvery grey hairs which help to protect the plant by reflecting some of the strong sunlight. It lives without flowering for many years, then produces a mass of blooms at the end of a long stalk. After its seeds have ripened, the plant dies.

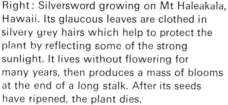

Although brown is a common plant colour, it is rather rare in flowers. The browns of this unusual South American orchid are probably caused by carotenoid pigments.

and less than 0.01mm in diameter. They are found in large numbers in the cells of leaves. Chlorophyll is also responsible for the green colour of other plant parts such as stems (as in cacti) and green fruits and seeds.

Some basically green plants often look greyish or bluish (called glaucous by botanists) and are favoured by gardeners for their special appearance. The subtle colour is produced when the outer plant surface is hairy or is covered by an outer layer of wax which modifies the green. In nature such plants are often found in sunny areas and their hairs and waxes may be a means of protecting the leaves from the effects of excessive sunlight, since they reflect a high proportion of it. Hairy surfaces also tend to reduce water loss from leaves.

Plants rarely if ever produce green by mixing blue and yellow pigments in the way that artists do. There are a few plants, however, where green pigments other than chlorophyll are used. An unknown pigment produces the verdigris green of the petals of the South African plant *Ixia viridiflora* and the common European wood-rotting fungus *Chlorosplenium aeruginescens* turns infected wood a bluish-green by producing a pigment called xylindeine.

Brown is the second most common colour in plants, often as the colour of old, dead tissue. Brown pigments are usually located in cell walls and are formed when plants are damaged, ageing or dead and their chemicals oxidise. They are seen, for instance, in the browning of a bruised apple and in the browns of autumn leaves. (Yellow and red autumn colours are, as we shall see, caused in different ways.) However, many plants have brown areas even when they are perfectly healthy. The brown scales of ferns, the brown roots of the Christmas rose and, of course, the brown barks of many trees are obvious examples.

In a few cases, like the bird's nest orchid and the broomrapes, small brown plastids, possibly coloured by brown carotenoid pigments, occur within the cells. Sometimes a plant has brown cell sap: the browns in the petals and sepals of some delphiniums and the *Coelogyne* group of orchids are caused in this way. In other cases brown is produced by pigments occurring together in the same cell – the combined effect of red cell sap with green chlorophyll, for example – or by separate pigments in cells lying one on top of the other.

Some plants become brown from a deposit of rust. This occurs around the roots of species growing in water-logged soils where the oxygen in the roots combines with the iron in the soil water to produce iron rust. Iron oxide incrustation is also known to cause browns in bacteria and algae.

Yellow flowers, such as the greater celandine and heartsease, are mostly coloured by plastid carotenoid pigments. In other yellow flowers, for example the primrose, vacuolar pigments such as anthoxanthin yellows dissolved in the cell sap are involved. It frequently needs a microscopic inspection to decide which means of pigmentation is employed in a yellow flower and sometimes both types may work together. Yellow pigments in cell walls are rarely important in flowers but give colour to certain leaves, woods and pollen grains. Pollen grains often owe their yellow to plastid carotenoid pigments as well as to cell wall pigments.

Plants that have been deprived of light are usually yellow. This happens because the green chlorophyll is unable to form properly in darkness: without light, only its yellow forerunner, protochlorophyll, can be formed in most plants. The yellow autumnal leaf colours shown spectacularly in so many trees in temperate parts of the world are caused when the chlorophyll-carrying chloroplasts break down in old age, producing droplets of yellow carotenoid pigments. The yellow autumnal leaves of the maidenhair tree and the golden leaves of the beech are familiar examples.

Orange can be produced by simple pigments or by the combined effect of different ones. Classic examples of simple pigments are the tomato and carrot, whose cells contain numerous small plastids with orange carotenoids. The orange of the corona or trumpet of certain *Narcissus*

Daffodils (above) and primroses (right) are among the first spring flowers in temperate regions. Yellow is a common flower colour, caused either by plastid carotenoid pigments or, as in primroses, by anthoxanthins in the cell sap. Yellow cell wall pigments are rare in flowers but colour some leaves, woods and pollen grains.

The bright scarlet of this double shrub rose 'Nina Weibull' is caused by red anthocyanin pigments dissolved in the cell sap. It was bred in 1962 from 'Fanal', a large, carmine-red semi-double floribunda, and 'Masquerade', a yellow rose that turns to pink and red as it ages.

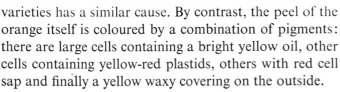

Left: The fruit of the orange tree changes colour as it ripens. The orange colour of the peel is caused by a combination of yellow oil, yellow-red plastids, red cell sap and a yellow waxy outer covering.

Right: Fallen maple leaves among pine needles. Autumn reds and yellows are caused by anthocyanins and carotenoids in cell sap. Brown pigments are usually in the cell walls and form when chemicals oxidize as the plant ages.

Left: Young oak leaves in spring. Red colours are quite common in young leaves and may possibly protect them against ultra-violet light. They form a nice contrast with the better known autumn colours.

varieties has a similar cause. By contrast, the peel of the orange itself is coloured by a combination of pigments: there are large cells containing a bright yellow oil, other cells containing yellow-red plastids, others with red cell sap and finally a yellow waxy covering on the outside.

The orange flower of the garden nasturtium is produced by red cell sap plus yellow plastid pigments within the cells. This type of combination is much commoner than a yellow cell sap/red plastid combination. Orange can also be caused if yellow anthoxanthin and red anthocyanin mix in the same cell or if these two pigments occur in separate overlying cell layers.

Red is very common in the plant kingdom and can be produced in a great variety of ways. The most frequent

24

is by vacuolar anthocyanin pigments dissolved in the cell sap as in flowers of garden geraniums, red delphiniums, red roses and paeonies. Amongst red vegetables radishes have a narrow layer of anthocyanin-containing cells, whilst in beetroot the sap of all the cells contains this type of red pigment. Many fruits are also coloured by anthocyanins, including grapes, plums and sweet cherries.

In leaves, red anthocyanin pigments may be produced in response to a variety of conditions. Sometimes, for no obvious reasons, plants produce them in frosty weather or when they are poorly supplied with phosphorus. In autumn it is anthocyanins that turn the leaves red when their chlorophyll has been broken down. Some living, healthy leaves have a high concentration of anthocyanins which may mask the green of the chlorophyll completely as in the copper beech or partially as in many variegated house plants – *Begonia* species and *Coleus blumei* for example.

Red plastid pigments are rather rare but cause, among others, the redness of hips (the fruit of *Rosa* species) and the redder varieties of tomatoes.

Blue anthocyanins are responsible for many flower blues, such as those of flax, cornflowers, blue delphiniums and gentians. Blue anthocyanin pigments are chemically similar to red anthocyanins and so it is not surprising that a number of species have varieties with red and blue flowers. Sometimes colour changes can occur within the same flower.

When it is extracted from the plant, a typical anthocyanin turns red in acid and blue in alkaline solution but it is not clear how much changes in the acidity of the cell sap affect flower colours in nature. We know, however, that bluebells can be turned red if their flowers are plunged into ant hills; the ants' defensive juices are acid enough to turn the pigment from blue to red. An old gardening trick is to sprinkle red hydrangeas with aluminium or iron alum solution to change their colour to blue. The added chemical changes the colour not by influencing cell sap acidity but by combining with the anthocyanin to give a new, blue pigment.

Other blue pigments are rare, but one intriguing example is the way certain fungi, e.g. *Boletus cyanescens*, turn blue when they are damaged. This is caused by a chemical change that occurs when a normally white or colourless substance in the fungi is exposed to air and converted to a blue pigment.

Violet colours may be produced directly from violet anthocyanins or by a combination of red and blue pigments in different layers of cells. Occasionally, unknown cell wall pigments produce violet colours, as in some

Some fungi, such as this *Boletus cyanescens*, turn blue when they are damaged and a normally white or colourless substance in the soft, pithy inside is exposed to the air. By a chemical change, the colourless substance is converted to a pigment which colours the fungus blue.

pollen grains. Scientists believe that many blue and mauve garden flowers owe their colours to 'co-pigmentation', a special combination of an anthocyanin pigment and an anthoxanthin. In some unknown way the anthoxanthin does not give a colour itself but causes the anthocyanin to go more bluish.

Black is caused in a great variety of ways. There may simply be a dense concentration of very dark anthocyanins in the cell sap, as in the black parts of the petals of garden pansies and the black berries of privet. In other cases there is a combination of pigments. Black currants have violet anthocyanins which, when combined with the green of the seed coat, look black. In poppies the black parts are caused by an intense purple anthocyanin pigmentation with curious blue granules underneath. Mysterious black solids of varying chemical compositions occur within the cells of some species and colour the black buds of the ash tree and the black wood of ebony. Sometimes cell walls are black while the cell contents are colourless. This occurs in many ferns, in the glossy mid-ribs of the fronds of the common spleenwort for example, and the black underground stem of bracken. Many fungi have black cell wall pigments. One of these, tar spot disease, occurs commonly on sycamore trees but apparently causes little harm. The conspicuous tar-like band seen at low tide on rocky seashores is the black of the walls of millions of cells of lichens of *Verrucaria* species.

Whites can be produced by white pigments dissolved in cell sap – white anthoxanthins. These occur, for example, in both common and wild chamomile. White can also be produced by physical effects, even when there is no chemical pigmentation. Sometimes they are due to air spaces within the plant's tissue, where the refraction and reflection of light makes it look white. The whiteness of linen, foam and snow, which is made up of colourless ice crystals and air spaces, have a similar cause. Ice, without air spaces, is not white but colourless. Examples of this kind of physical white are the flowers of white water lilies, white chrysanthemums and the white or silvery blotches on the leaves of many variegated house plants such as the aluminium plant, *Pilea cadieri*. The white of the edelweiss is caused by refraction and reflection from the mass of colourless hairs which cover the plant.

The reflection of ultra-violet light by flowers which, we shall see, is so important for bees and other insects, is brought about without the aid of chemical pigments. The outer layer of cells of many flowers have a special fine structure which reflects ultra-violet. This occurs whether they have chemical pigments or not, and is known in

Left: Many plants produce anthocyanins when conditions are unfavourable. Red colours, for example, often indicate a lack of phosphorus. Herb robert develops red colours very easily, here perhaps in response to unusually dry conditions.

Right: Blue anthocyanin pigments in the cell sap give delphiniums their colour. Blue and red anthocyanin pigments are chemically similar and many blue flowers, including delphiniums, have red varieties.

The attractive blue 'berries' of this juniper are not true berries but special cones, since junipers are conifers not flowering plants. Nevertheless their colour and fleshiness attract animals to disperse the seeds.

Left: The 'colour' of water lily flowers is not caused by a chemical pigment but by air spaces within the plant's tissue. These cause light to be reflected and refracted but since no wavelength is absorbed more than another, the petals appear white.

27

The white rays of mayweed are coloured chemically by white pigments dissolved in cell sap. Because the pigments absorb all light wavelengths equally, no colour is produced.

The surface cells of gloxinia petals have tiny projections. The massed effect of their countless numbers gives the petals their beautiful velvety texture.

The glossy sheen of buttercup petals increases the flower's attraction to pollinating insects. It is caused by a layer of cells, full of highly reflective starch grains, which act like a mirror underneath the yellow pigmented cells.

Left: Tree barks can have a wide range of colours, ranging from black through red to white. Among the most spectacular are the aspens, which owe their characteristic white trunks to air spaces in the outer bark and have no chemical white pigments.

good example. An exceptionally beautiful effect is seen in the iridescent peacock flower of South Africa, which has a remarkable gloss. Unfortunately we do not know exactly how this is produced. Many seaweeds, particularly those that grow in warmer seas, are also iridescent. Their iridescence seems somehow to be caused by the effects of light on unusual solids in their surface cells.

Less mysterious is the curious, oily sheen of the buttercup. Buttercup petals have an outer layer of cells which are very smooth and filled with a yellow oily solution. Beneath these is a layer of cells densely packed with white starch grains, which give a maximum reflection of light. The combination of these layers gives the shiny brightness and intense yellow colour.

The physical structure of its outer petal layers can alter the intensity of a flower's colouration. Sometimes pale colours are merely the result of a very dilute pigment within the cell, or a small number of deeply pigmented cells in a mass of colourless tissue. Paleness can also be caused by air spaces. A good example of this is the pale blue flower of flax which has loosely packed outer cells and air spaces overlying the pigmented zones. Only near the veins are the outer cells packed more tightly and here the blue colour is highlighted.

Plant colours and evolution

It is a characteristic of plants that they possess green chlorophyll and other pigments to capture sunlight. Though plant colours are not preserved in fossil remains, it is therefore reasonable to assume that by the time life had evolved into light-using plants, some 3,000 million years ago, they were already green. In simpler plants the use of colours is still largely restricted to capturing sunlight and although they may possess a range of other pigments these are considered to be merely waste products.

During evolution, however, plant reproduction became more complex and as flowering plants developed, colours fulfilled another function, acting as signals to attract the animals which move pollen, seeds or fruit. Again, it is not possible to say exactly when and why these secondary uses of colour developed but the laws of natural selection make it clear that the colours of flowering plants that attracted the right animals most successfully are the ones that have survived. With the arrival of agricultural man, another major factor directly influenced plant colours: the selection of plants for ornaments.

These functions of plant colours in harnessing light, summoning animals and as ornaments for man provide the framework for the rest of this book.

yellow flowers (e.g. lesser celandine), red flowers (e.g. field poppy) and blue flowers (e.g. borage). Ultra-violet light can also be *absorbed* by a number of pigments: white anthoxanthins, for example, absorb ultra-violet light strongly.

The numerous special textural effects and glosses which occur in plants have both physical and chemical causes. The velvety sheen so noticeable on many petals, like those of the hothouse gloxinia, is caused because the outer layer of cells has countless minute projections. Where these projections are large enough to be called hairs there is a silky or silvery lustre, like that of the beautiful ice plant with its so-called drop or water sheen. A perfectly smooth outer layer of cells gives a different sheen – the polished leaves of the indiarubber plant are a

Photosynthesis: how plants use sunlight

The most important colour in plants, and indeed in the whole world, is the green of chlorophyll. It is this pigment that harnesses sunlight and channels its energy into producing the chemicals and oxygen that provide for all life on earth.

In the sun, 148 million kilometres away, a continuous nuclear explosion is going on. The enormous energy this produces is radiated as electromagnetic waves in all directions across space. A tiny fraction (equivalent nonetheless to the energy produced by one million atom bombs) reaches the outer part of the earth's atmosphere every day. Over a third of this is reflected back into space by clouds, snow and ice. Most of the remainder warms up the oceans and the land and drives the great heat engine of the earth which we recognize as weather. A small amount of the energy, light mainly in the red and blue region of the visible spectrum, is absorbed by the chlorophyll of green plants. (Green light is the least *absorbed* by green plants; we see their transmitted or reflected light.) By a process called photosynthesis some of this light is converted into the chemical energy of the plants' substance. The earth's plants trap in this way on average about 0.2% of the energy of the sun's radiation that reaches the earth's surface.

Harvesting of sunlight only takes place in chlorophyll-containing green plant cells (minor exceptions to this are discussed later). In photosynthesis, the chlorophyll captures the energy of sunlight and uses it to split water into its constituents hydrogen and oxygen and to form energy-rich compounds. The hydrogen is combined with other chemicals in the plant, but much of the oxygen is liberated into the air because the plant does not use all of it. The plant uses the chemicals it has formed to help convert carbon dioxide into carbohydrates and other organic matter. These spread throughout the plant to be

Dense montane forest in Ecuador. Green is the most important colour for plants and animals alike. It is not clear why there is not just one green and the subtle differences of colour in a tropical forest may be a feature of very precise adaptations by plants The species with paler green leaves may, for example, benefit from the decreased light and therefore heat which they absorb in intense sunlight.

used for growth, seed and fruit production. Given sunlight, green plants are thus able to form all the chemical compounds they need from the gas carbon dioxide in the atmosphere, water and small quantities of mineral salts from the soil. (The mineral salts include nitrates, phosphates and potassium salts, the basis of farm and garden fertilizers.)

The main by-product of photosynthesis, oxygen, is of overwhelming importance to all other living things and has made life on land possible. Plants, virtually alone, have produced the oxygen which now forms a large proportion of our atmosphere. Green plants in the sea were making oxygen over 3,000 million years ago. Very slowly the oxygen content of the atmosphere increased and after millions of years, perhaps 450 million years ago, life on land began.

The reason for the long period of life in the sea before life on land evolved is closely connected with oxygen. When it reaches the upper layer of the atmosphere, some of the oxygen is converted to the gas ozone, which blocks the ultra-violet radiation sent out by the sun and prevents it from reaching the earth's surface. Until sufficient oxygen and its product ozone had been produced by the green plants, the lethal radiation reaching the earth would have killed any living organisms on land. Ultra-violet radiation does not penetrate water, so plants and animals were able to evolve safely in the depths of the ocean, gradually emerging to colonize the land when there was enough oxygen and ozone to reduce ultra-violet radiation to an acceptable level.

Plant chemical energy in the form of green plants is therefore the very thread of life on earth. The rest of the living world, including animals and fungi, cannot use light to manufacture their own substances. Instead they obtain the plant chemical energy, which we call food, in a great variety of ways. Some, called herbivores, eat the green plants directly. Others, called carnivores, feed on herbivores and other carnivores. Parasites obtain their food by living on or in green plants, herbivores or carnivores. Many animals (including man) feed on both green plants and other animals, and are said to be omnivores.

Even after they have died, plants continue to be useful. Together with decaying animal matter they provide food for a whole battery of decomposer organisms, including small animals, fungi and bacteria. Since plant substances that are eaten can only be used efficiently if they are combined with oxygen in the body, we are doubly dependent on plants: they provide both the raw materials and the oxygen for releasing their energy to maintain the living world.

All animals are dependent either directly or indirectly on plants for their food. Herbivores are primary consumers, living entirely on plants. Carnivores, including parasites, are secondary consumers, feeding on animals that have eaten plants. Fungi, small insects and bacteria feed on dead and decaying plants and animals. Man, an omnivore, is both a primary and a secondary consumer. As a herbivore he eats mainly grains and vegetables; his main food crops are cultivated over vast areas of the world's surface. As a carnivore he is at a higher stage in the food chain. Because energy is lost at each stage, man's use of animals as a food source is inefficient.

Plant materials can be burned at high temperatures, when their energy is given off mainly as heat. This is the principle of fossil fuel burning on which we depend for much of our industrial and domestic energy requirements. Oil, coal and peat are products of ancient photosynthesis and by burning them we release energy captured by green chlorophyll from sunlight millions of years ago.

When plant materials are consumed by burning or respiration the materials that remain are the same as those required for photosynthesis: carbon dioxide and water. It must not be thought, however, that burning and respiration are a simple reversal of photosynthesis. The chemical pathways by which these processes occur are actually quite different.

In land plants photosynthesis takes place mainly in the leaves. The basic requirements are: water, carbon dioxide and sunlight. Water absorbed by the roots enters the leaf through the xylem system. Carbon dioxide from the air enters through the stomata in the leaf's surface. Sunlight penetrates the translucent outer layer of cells. Inside the leaf, the water is split into its components, hydrogen and oxygen, using the energy of sunlight. The oxygen then returns to the atmosphere through the stomata. By a complicated chemical process the hydrogen combines with the carbon dioxide to make sugars.

12 molecules of water brought into the leaf by the xylem. Each molecule contains 2 hydrogen atoms + 1 oxygen atom.

1 molecule of glucose which contains all the carbon and half the oxygen from the carbon dioxide, and half the hydrogen from the water. This is used as a source of energy for the plant.

hydrogen
oxygen
carbon

6 molecules of oxygen released from the leaf into the atmosphere. Each molecule contains 2 atoms of oxygen.

6 molecules of water produced by the chemical reaction and available for further use by the plant.

6 molecules of carbon dioxide enter the leaf through the stomata. Each molecule contains 2 atoms of oxygen + 1 atom of carbon

The discovery of photosynthesis

The key, light-trapping role of plants was not recognized until relatively recently in the history of human thought. Aristotle and the other Greeks observed that the life processes of animals were dependent on the food that they ate and assumed that plants took the food they needed from the soil. The true source of plant nourishment was gradually discovered by the early scientific chemists.

Around 1660 Johann Baptist van Helmont provided a convincing demonstration that soil alone does not nourish plants. He grew a small willow tree in a pot for five years and added only rainwater or distilled water. The tree increased in weight by about 80kg over this period while the soil lost only about 50g. Van Helmont understandably though mistakenly believed that the increased weight of the willow was due entirely to water.

In 1771 Joseph Priestley, an English clergyman, made another experiment that was to lead to the understanding of what makes plants grow. He placed a candle under a glass dome and allowed it to burn up all the oxygen in the air. When it had gone out because there was no oxygen left, he put a shoot of mint under the dome. After a few days he was able to light the candle again – oxygen had been restored to the air. The essential role of light in this restoration of oxygen to the air was discovered a few years later by the Dutch scientist Jan Ingenhouz. Finally a Frenchman, de Saussure was able to prove that plants obtain water from the soil and carbon dioxide from the air and convert these raw materials into plant matter and oxygen in sunlight. The precise details of photosynthesis are still the subject of much botanical research although a great deal has been discovered over the last thirty years or so.

The mechanism of photosynthesis

When pigments absorb light they absorb its energy, which they re-emit in various ways. Very often the absorbed light makes the pigment warmer than its surroundings and the light energy is sent out as heat. Sometimes part of the energy is converted into light of a longer wavelength and the pigment is then said to fluoresce. Chlorophyll, the pigment which absorbs light energy for photosynthesis, only functions efficiently if it is arranged in a very precise way inside the plant, and is connected to the rest of the plant's mechanisms for converting sunlight and carbon dioxide into plant substances. In order to understand this arrangement properly it is necessary to learn some elementary points of plant anatomy.

In the majority of land plants most photosynthesis occurs in the leaves. The cells inside a leaf are joined together but there are air spaces in between. The outermost or epidermal layers are continuous and are perforated with holes called stomata. It is through these holes that the inner parts of the leaf remain in contact with the air outside: through them carbon dioxide is taken in and oxygen given out. Stomata are controlled by special cells called guard cells which surround the openings. Some water is inevitably lost through the stomata, so control is crucial if the plant is not to desiccate in dry conditions.

The chloroplasts which contain the pigment chlorophyll are found inside the inner cells of the leaf and also inside the guard cells of the epidermis. It is here that photosynthesis actually takes place. Through an electron microscope it is possible to see that inside the tiny chloroplasts are even smaller, flattened hollow bodies called thylakoids. These are grouped in stacks called grana. The chlorophyll is on the walls of the thylakoids, while the other substances important in photosynthesis are in the minute spaces between them. Whilst there are exceptions to these anatomical arrangements (the tiny photosynthetic bacteria and blue-green algae, for example, have no chloroplasts), the chlorophyll is always arranged in a definite way.

Chloroplasts do not stay still within leaf cells but are able to move in response to light. In dim light they tend to move close to the cell walls facing the light so that they can absorb as much as possible. In strong light they

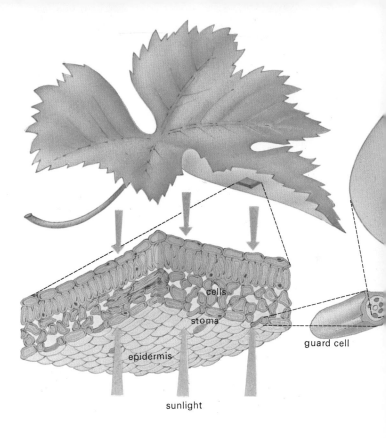

move towards the cell walls that lie in the plane of the oncoming light and turn their edges to the sun. This helps protect them from the effects of too *much* sunlight.

An important group of land plants has evolved a refined system of photosynthesis by which they are able to take up carbon dioxide about three times as rapidly as other plants. The details of the system are rather complex but the plants can be easily recognized under a microscope because they have sheaths of chloroplast rich cells surrounding the veins in the leaves. Examples of these so-called efficient plants are maize and sugar cane.

Some bacteria are also able to photosynthesize, using infra-red light and pigments related to chlorophyll. Infrared light has a longer wavelength than the light used by green plants and is of lower energy. Bacteria are able to use it because their type of photosynthesis usually involves splitting hydrogen sulphide and this requires much less energy than the plant's usual splitting of water (hydrogen oxide).

Quite recently it has been discovered that there is one remarkable exception to the idea that all photosynthesizing cells contain chlorophyll. The bacterium *Halobacterium halobium* uses a coloured protein rather like the visual pigment of animal eyes (rhodopsin) to capture sunlight for photosynthesis.

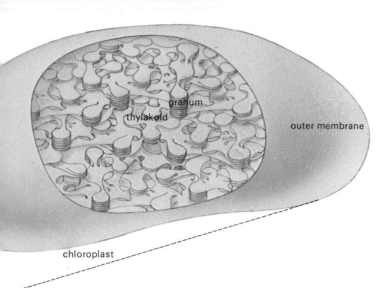

granum

thylakoid

outer membrane

chloroplast

Photosynthesis can only take place in plants containing chlorophyll, the important light-trapping green pigment. Chlorophyll is found in the guard cells around the stomata as well as in the inner cells. It is contained in chloroplasts, tiny plastids mainly between 4 to 6 microns across (1 micron is 1 millionth of a metre). Inside the chloroplasts are even smaller structures, the thylakoids, arranged in stacks, the grana. Chlorophyll is on the walls of the thylakoids and traps light to provide the energy for the reactions which turn carbon dioxide and water to sugars.

This microscopic enlargement of part of a maize leaf shows the layer of cells surrounding the water conducting pipes or vascular bundles. In maize (and many other plants which grow in warmer countries) the cells around the vascular bundles in the leaves contain large numbers of special chloroplasts. These are associated with a 'super-efficient' photosynthetic mechanism. This leaf has stomata on both the upper and lower surfaces.

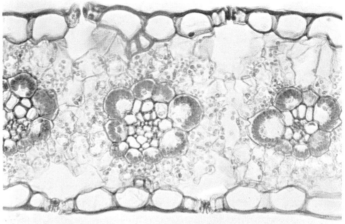

The pigments of seaweeds are often different from those of land plants. Red seaweeds do contain chlorophyll but they have additional red pigments which are thought to adapt them to life in deeper water, where they can absorb the predominantly blue light. A number of red species also occur near the top of the tidal zone Green seaweeds have similar pigments to those of land plants and are much less common in deeper water.

Photosynthesis and non-green plants

There are, of course, many plants that are not green. In some of these, the chlorophyll pigment is hidden but it is still used for photosynthesis. Conspicuous non-green plants occur on rocky shores throughout the world – the brown and red rockweeds or seaweeds. Brown seaweeds contain a brown carotenoid pigment, red seaweeds a water soluble red pigment and these give them their characteristic colours. These pigments often mask the green chlorophyll while the plants are alive but when they are cast on the shore and die the brown and red pigments decompose more quickly and the chlorophyll shows through.

Why should seaweeds have these additional pigments? The answer lies partly in the light absorbing characteristics of the sea (all seaweeds are covered by sea, at least at high tides). Red light is very rapidly absorbed by water and even at relatively shallow depths water appears blue. This means that light reaching submerged plants has much less red in its composition than light received by land plants. The brown and red pigments absorb the blue light more efficiently than green pigments and are able to transfer the extra energy they gather to chlorophyll, which then directs it through the same chemical processes that occur in green plants.

Some seaweeds have no additional pigments, only the same green chlorophyll as land plants. These green seaweeds are found in the higher parts of the tidal zone and because their pigments are so similar, it is believed that they are related to the ancestors of the true land plants. The brown and red seaweeds have no known descendants among land plants.

Another category of plants that are not green are the parasites. These maintain and reproduce themselves not by harnessing light in photosynthesis but by using the energy of other living organisms. Amongst flowering plants they range from the fine, twining dodders to the spectacular *Rafflesia arnoldii* of Sumatra, which has the largest flowers in the world. Parasitic flowering plants have evolved from green ancestors and now feed by sending suckers into their host's tissue to obtain nutrients and water. Some parasites, such as the mistletoes, are green and obtain some of their food for themselves, the rest from their host. They are often called hemi- or half-parasites for this reason.

Some flowering plants live off the dead remains of other plants. All orchids, without exception, do this in the early stages of their life. They obtain their food not

Plants without chlorophyll.
The twining stems of this rootless parasitic dodder bear no chlorophyll-containing leaves. Instead, it absorbs water and all the food it needs from its host. Mistletoes (right) are partial parasites. They have green leaves so carry out some photosynthesis, but they obtain water and mineral nutrients from the host tree. Fungi such as the fly agaric (below left) live on decaying plant and animal matter and do not photosynthesize. In this case, the bright colour may be a warning to animals that they are poisonous. A special fungus grows at the root of the colourless bird's nest orchid (below), passing on food through a joint organ called a mycorrhiza.

directly from dead plants but through an intermediary, a fungus which dissolves the dead matter and passes it on to the orchid. This is an example of a mycorrhizal relationship between a higher plant and a fungus. The orchid seedling is never green but, depending on the species, it may become green as it grows and will then be able to photosynthesize for itself. Adult orchids range from those that are probably completely free living, like the slipper orchid and others with large green leaves, to the bird's nest and coral root orchids which never possess chlorophyll and emerge above ground as whitish spikes of flowers. There is at least one species that grows completely underground, flowers, fruits and all, the Australian *Rhizanthella gardneri*.

The fungi are a group of plants which never contain chlorophyll and are always parasitic or decompose dead matter. Although they are usually studied by botanists they differ in so many ways from green plants that they are now often considered to be a separate kingdom of the living world. Indeed, it is still not certain if the fungi have evolved from animal or plant ancestors.

The only parts of fungi which we normally see are the fruit bodies, for example toadstools and brackets. These fruit bodies are actually clumps or groups of fine fungal threads which spread invisibly through the materials that form their food. The fruit bodies produce reproductive spores and disperse them into the air, mostly by using little explosive devices. They are then blown about by air currents. The brightly coloured fruit bodies of fungi are one of a number of cases where we cannot be certain of the function of a colour in nature. It may be that in some cases they advertise a bad-tasting or poisonous substance which discourages animals from eating them.

A remarkable example of fungi which apparently feed themselves are the lichens, many of which are brightly coloured. In these plants the fungal body or thallus can be seen growing on soil, tree bark or often bare rock without decomposing it in any way. The answer to the mystery of how the lichen lives without consuming plant or animal matter can be seen if it is examined under a microscope.

Inside the body of the lichen are tiny cells of an alga which have chlorophyll and are able to trap light and use its energy. The green of the chlorophyll is often masked by other pigments whose purpose remains mysterious. The lichen is, then, one of the most perfect examples known of mutualism, where two unrelated organisms provide benefits for each other. The fungus provides the alga with a safe place to live while in return it receives food from the alga's photosynthesis. So successful is this mutualism that lichens grow further north, further

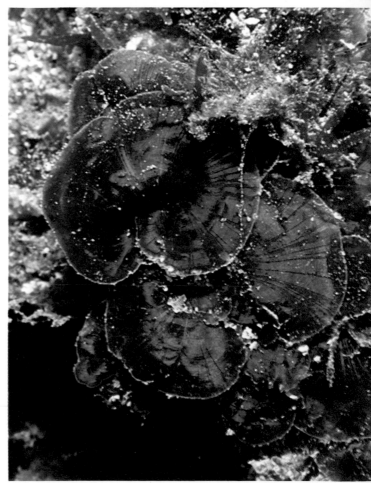

Left: Two species of lichens (orange *Xanthoria* and grey-green *Ramalina*) on a rocky shore. Lichens are dual organisms. The main body is a fungus but unlike other fungi it does not feed on decaying matter. Within its tissues (below) are chlorophyll-containing cells of a green or blue-green alga. These photosynthesize and provide food for the fungus. In return, the fungus provides the alga with a safe place to live. Very often lichens are brightly coloured by pigments which mask the green chlorophyll.

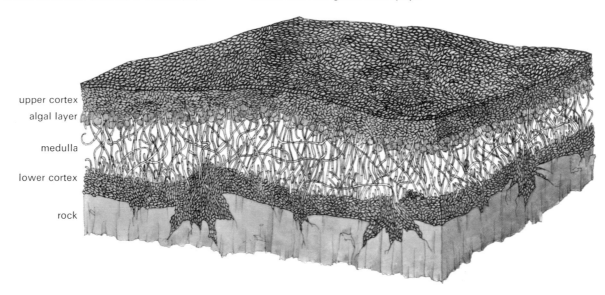

upper cortex
algal layer
medulla
lower cortex
rock

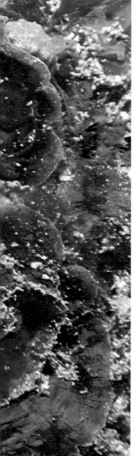

Light-producing toadstool *Poromycena manipularis* from Sarawak. Many fungi are luminous and rotting wood in forests often shows a ghostly phosphorescence at night. In the tropical forests of Sarawak some fungi produce light bright enough to read by.

This blue, iridescent seaweed is common in many Australian seas, but the function of its unusual colour has not yet been explained. The specimen here was collected at 20m off the coast of New South Wales and has still to be classified.

south and at higher altitudes than any other type of plants that are visible to the naked human eye.

Plants that produce light

It is appropriate to mention in this chapter those groups of plants that are able to reverse the general process of light absorption by the vegetable kingdom and to produce light. The phenomenon of bioluminescence, well known amongst animals such as glow-worms, fire-flies and deep sea fish occurs also in plants. Examples can be found in some microscopic marine algae which give out light when they come into contact with oxygen and provide a scintillating display on the crests of breaking waves. They may also produce light when they are disturbed by boats passing through the water; even fish and human swimmers have been surrounded by halos of light! One of these luminescent plants, *Gonyaulax*, may be so abundant in sheltered bays when conditions are right that the whole water surface glows. *Gonyaulax* is one of the algae responsible for the sinister 'coloured seas' where millions of the tiny plants turn the water red or orange by day. They are very poisonous, and accumulate in the shellfish which fish eat. This can result in the deaths of masses of fish.

Some fungi are also bioluminescent. The light given off by rotting wood, known since the time of the ancient Greeks, is caused by certain species of fungi which are breaking down the wood. In some fungi the whole fruiting body may glow. In both algae and fungi the light-producing mechanism involves a substance called luciferin (whose exact chemical constitution varies) which is 'burned' in the presence of a special enzyme, luciferase, by the oxygen in the air. The burning takes place at low temperatures, of course, and causes the light.

Though we know how plants produce light, no-one has yet explained why they do so. Some authors have claimed that light-producing fungi attract flies which disperse the spores. This is, however, unlikely, for the parts of the fungus that glow most brightly are often the parts that do not produce spores at all. The process of light production is so complex and involved that it seems certain that it has some real purpose yet to be discovered.

Pigments that affect growth

Some pigments occur in such small quantities in a plant that they are invisible to us. Whilst they can hardly be termed a plant colour in the usual sense they do absorb light of certain wavelengths and have a vitally important influence on plant growth.

The best known of these pigments is the mysterious phytochrome which has only recently been purified and had its chemical composition worked out. Phytochrome is a protein which absorbs red light and though it occurs in tiny quantities (about 1 gramme in a hundred tonnes of leaves) it nevertheless has effects on many apparently unrelated aspects of plant life.

It is a common experience for gardeners to find that when the soil is turned over, weed seeds begin to sprout on the surface. The light somehow triggers the germination of the seeds which have been stored in the soil. It is easy to see that this is very advantageous for the plants, since if they began to grow in the dark sublayers they might never reach the light. The pigment phytochrome, which occurs in the seed surface, apparently controls this reaction.

Phytochrome exists in two forms, Pr and Pfr. It is the second form, Pfr, which acts as a biochemical trigger on the seed and causes it to germinate. While the seed is in the dark, there is not enough Pfr to have any effect. When the pigment is exposed to light, however, the Pr form begins to change into the active Pfr form and as soon as this is present in sufficient quantities, the seed begins to sprout.

Phytochrome may also control the shape of plants. For example plants that are grown in total darkness have a characteristic pattern of growth: they are long and slender, yellowish with small leaves. In the light, phytochrome probably helps to control normal growth by triggering the production of essential chemicals, in-

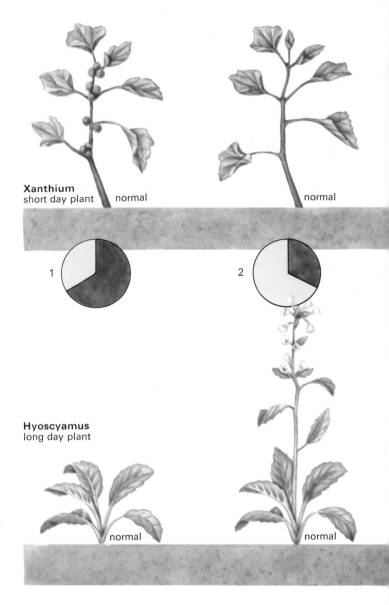

Xanthium short day plant — normal — normal

Hyoscyamus long day plant — normal — normal

cluding chlorophyll. Without light, the phytochrome remains inactive.

Another very important function of phytochrome in many plants is that it enables them to tell what time of year it is. Without a sense of time many plants would face disaster. Imagine the consequences if trees came into leaf on the first warm day of spring, only to lose their leaves in a later frost. To some extent the annual cycles of growth are regulated by cycles of temperature but this is too crude for many purposes. The infallible guide to the annual cycles is the length of the day, which

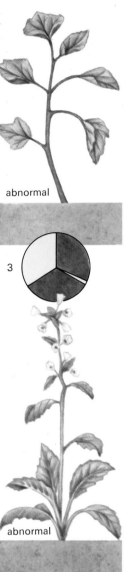

abnormal

3

abnormal

Plants sense the seasons of the year partly by temperature and partly by measuring the changing day lengths. Some plants, known as short day plants, only flower when there are less than a certain number of hours of daylight. Others, known as long day plants, need more than a certain number of daylight hours before they will flower. Plants apparently measure the length of the dark rather than the light periods and their flowering times can be regulated by interrupting the darkness with even a brief flash of light.

The illustration shows a short day plant (Xanthium) and a long day plant (Hyoscyamus) at three different times:

1. During a short day with 8 hours of light.

2. During a long day with 16 hours of light.

3. During a short day when the darkness was interrupted by a flash of artificial light.

The short day plant needs 15½ hours of light or less to bloom, so flowers in (1) but not in (2). It would normally flower on a day with only 8 hours of light (3) but has been prevented from doing so by the flash of light. The long day plant does not flower until (2), as it needs at least 10 hours of light. It would not normally flower on a short day (3) but the flash of light interrupting the darkness has upset its timing mechanism and it has produced flowers.

changes in exactly the same way year after year. For many years it has been known that plants (and animals) can measure the day length and hence follow the seasons accurately.

This phenomenon is called photoperiodism and its best studied aspect in plants is the regulation of flowering. An understanding of flowering is of great importance for the gardener or farmer who wants to prevent plants from channelling their energies into producing flowers so that he can use their leaves or underground parts as crops. Horticulturists may, of course, also wish to make plants flower at an unusual time, for example to produce flowers for special occasions in winter.

Many plants, such as tomatoes, flower irrespective of daylength, providing they have enough light for growth. But there are large numbers of plants which will not flower without their correct daylength. Most of these fall into two categories: long day plants which must be exposed to daylength over a certain number of hours before they will flower and short day plants which will only flower when the light period is less than a certain number of hours. Other plants have more complicated requirements of daylength and sometimes even varieties of the same species (tobacco for example) differ.

Both wild and cultivated plants of north temperate regions usually flower in summer and not surprisingly include many long day plants such as clovers, spinach, and sugarbeet. Short day plants are characteristic of countries further south and include crops such as soya beans, hemp and globe artichokes. Tropical equatorial plants are not affected by daylength since annual changes in temperature and daylight are very slight.

Experimental studies have shown that plants measure the length of the night rather than the length of the day. Flowering in a short day plant can be prevented by interrupting a long night with a flash of light. A long day plant can be deceived into flowering at the wrong time of year by the same method. Interrupting the length of day with a short period of darkness has no effect. The full explanation of the mechanism of photoperiodism has still not been discovered but it is certain that phytochrome is involved at least in the initial perception of the light.

Another photoperiodic process in which phytochrome is probably involved is the laying down of bulbs and tubers for winter food storage. It is also believed that small quantities of the pigment occur in the surface of the resting buds of deciduous trees. The pigment perceives the light and sends appropriate signals when it is time for the leaves to break in spring.

An unknown pigment is involved in the bending and twisting movements plants make in response to light. Anyone who has grown plants on window ledges will know that they turn their leaves in the direction in which they will obtain most light. Growth towards light is crucially important in nature since competing plants tend to shade each other out. Much scientific work has been done on the bending of grass seedlings towards light shining from the side and it seems that close to the tip of the plant there is a pigment that is sensitive to light. When this is stimulated it causes a chemical message to be sent down the plant to bend it towards the light.

The role of flowers in the life of a plant

Flowers are the specialized organs of plants used for the production and dispersal of seeds. This definition is rather different from the popular meaning of the word 'flower', which people often use to describe a plant that has attractive blooms. The more accurate definition is also more comprehensive: it applies to inconspicuous flowers like those of grasses and trees as well as to those of more obviously showy garden plants.

Flowers produce pollen grains (which we can think of as male cells) and eggs (female cells). These are often both produced within the same flower but most plants have some way of moving pollen from their own flowers to the flowers of other plants. The movement of pollen is called pollination – cross-pollination when separate plants are involved and self-pollination when pollen is transferred within a single flower or between different flowers on the same plant. In nature there is a complete spectrum of plants ranging from those which are totally self-pollinated through those which have a balance of both methods to plants which are totally cross-pollinated. When growing plants it is useful to know how pollination is achieved, for most flowers, if not pollinated, will produce no seeds or fruit.

The transferred pollen grain settles onto a receptive surface called the stigma, where it germinates and produces a pollen tube. The stigma is actually the tip of the ovary, inside which is the ovule containing the female egg cell. The pollen tube grows towards the egg cell, entering the ovule through a special hole called the micropyle. Inside the ovule the pollen tube discharges two cells which have travelled down it from the pollen grain. One of these fuses with the egg cell to start the embryo plant; the second male cell fuses with other cells to make tissue which will provide the growing embryo with food.

The petals of a lotus flower change from rose red to yellowish as they grow older. After the petals drop, the seed pod (right) enlarges greatly, turns from green to brown and eventually droops over to discharge the seeds in the water. The pods may float upside down for some time, dispersing the seeds over a wider area.

After fertilization, the parts of the ovule surrounding the embryo plant mature and its outer walls harden until eventually it is recognizable as the seed. As the seed hardens the ovary wall also develops and produces the fruit wall. Sometimes an ovary may contain several ovules. In this case each ovule must be fertilized by a separate pollen grain and will then develop into a separate seed within the single fruit.

How flowers are pollinated

Plants, unlike animals, cannot move about to find a suitable mate. Instead they have to rely on outside forces to move their pollen for them. They use three basic agents to do this: water, wind and animals.

Sea grasses are some of only a few plants which are specially adapted to water pollination. Colour does not play any part in achieving the pollen movement so plants that use water have flowers which are greenish and inconspicuous. Most aquatic plants, however, produce flowers above water and use the wind or animals to move their pollen.

Wind pollination, by contrast, is very common, particularly amongst plants in temperate parts of the world. Again, colours are not important so the flowers of wind-pollinated plants are small and dull. How many people notice the flowers of oak, ash or beech trees? Nevertheless many of these small blooms are beautifully marked and coloured, although the colour has no obvious function. The vivid reds of the female hazel catkin and the duller reds of ripening elm flowers are welcome colours in the brown woodlands of early spring. In some cases, for example male hazel catkins, there is so much pollen on a wind-pollinated flower that its colour becomes very conspicuous. Each grain is so tiny that once the wind has blown them off the plant they are invisible to us, though they all too often make their presence felt to hayfever sufferers!

Plants which use animals to transfer their pollen must have some way of attracting them and so use colours to provide a signal that stands out against a background of green or brown. There must also be some reason for pollinators to continue calling at the flowers so the plants provide rewards in the form of food, either the pollen itself or nectar or occasionally other substances.

Nectar is a fluid which contains simple sugars and provides a rich source of energy for visiting animals. Recently it has been found that the nectar of many flowers contains small amounts of proteins or amino-acids which may be an important source of animal nutrition. Some nectars are poisonous or foul-tasting and it is known that in some cases butterflies can be discouraged in this

Grasses have inconspicuous flowers which are highly specialized for wind-pollination. Here flowers in both male and female stages can be seen. The male anthers dangle on long, pendulous filaments which are caught by the wind. The females have long feathery stigmas which increase their chances of catching wind-borne pollen.

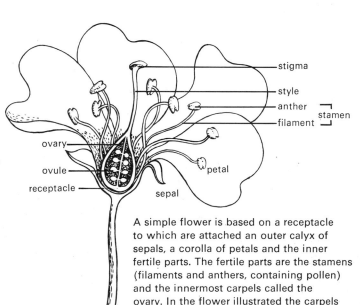

A simple flower is based on a receptacle to which are attached an outer calyx of sepals, a corolla of petals and the inner fertile parts. The fertile parts are the stamens (filaments and anthers, containing pollen) and the innermost carpels called the ovary. In the flower illustrated the carpels are fused together and are topped by a single style and stigma. Pollen settles on the stigma and the pollen tube grows down the style to reach the ovules inside the ovary.

Elm flowers bloom well before the tree comes into leaf. This is an advantage, as the leaves obstruct the wind on which the plant relies for pollination.

Left: A St. John's wort flower showing its free petals and numerous stamens with their filaments and anthers. The central ovary consists of five united carpels, each with a free style.

1 Petals are usually but not always a flower's main agent of attraction. In plants such as marsh marigolds the bright yellow sepals are the most conspicuous part of the flower.

2 The simplest flowers have separate petals, arranged in a shallow cup. However, many flowers have petals fused together into complex shapes. The snapdragon's shape is an adaptation to pollination by bees.

3 The sepal's usual role is to protect the bud and flower. Sometimes they also add to the flower's attraction: in tulips they are the same size, shape and colour as the petals.

4 Daisies belong to the Compositae family. The flower head is composed of hundreds of separate florets, central or tube florets and outer or ray florets. Each outer floret has one petal expanded into a ray.

5 The red sepals of the large flowered evening primrose contrast with its pale petals, making it more conspicuous to insects.

way from visiting and stealing nectar from flowers pollinated by bees.

Having attracted the animal pollinator, the flower needs some way of placing pollen onto it so that it can be transferred to the stigma of the next flower to be visited. For this reason the nectaries, which produce nectar, are strategically positioned to ensure the visitor comes into contact both with the anthers (which produce pollen) and the stigma (which receives it) while it is feeding.

Nectaries are in different positions in different types of flower. For example most flowers of plants belonging to the family Umbelliferae have nectar exposed on small open discs which are easily accessible to unspecialized short-tongued flies and small beetles. A scientist called Herman Müller studied one of these plants, the hogweed, and found that out of 118 species of insects visiting the flowers there were no butterflies and moths (which have long tongues). In contrast amongst the visitors to a dandelion flower, which conceals its nectar in a floral tube, there were more long- than short-tongued insects.

Sometimes concealed nectar reserved for special visitors is stolen by insects which reach the nectaries by biting through the flower. This, of course, completely bypasses any pollen transfer mechanism. It is often possible to find small neat holes at the bases of tubular flowers, the tell-tale evidence that an animal has taken nectar without performing any pollen distributing service.

Pollen itself can be eaten and often forms a food reward for animal visitors although some must always be left over for fertilization. It contains varying proportions of fats, carbohydrates and proteins and is therefore highly nutritious. People consume pollen, too, either with nectar in honey or sometimes processed on its own into pills, allegedly with remarkable powers of rejuvenation. The longevity of certain groups of people in Georgia and Peru has sometimes been ascribed to the pollen in their diet.

The structures of flowers

Because they have different pollination mechanisms, flowers vary greatly in structure and appearance from species to species. Some are immensely complex but there is a common basic structure. The outermost part of the flower is the calyx, composed of sepals which are frequently green. These protect the flower when it is in bud or sometimes even after it has opened. For example the tough calyx of thrift protects the inner part of the flower from thieving insects. In some flowers the calyx may be the most attractive part. This is the case in delphiniums, where the petals are transformed into

nectaries, and in marsh marigolds, which have very small petals or no petals at all. Other plants, such as fuchsias, have both sepals and petals attractively, and often contrastingly, coloured.

Within the calyx is the corolla of petals, which to the layman is the distinguishing part of most flowers. The chief role of petals is to attract pollinating animals and all their wide variety of scents, colours, shapes and sizes are associated with this. The simplest are like those of buttercups and poppies: oval, equal in size and shape, not joined together and arranged to give a shallow cup. Many plants have petals which are fused together and have very specialized shapes; the popular *Calceolaria* species are good examples.

Left: The giant hogweed is a spectacular member of the family Umbelliferae, and often grows to a height of 5 m. In this family the flowers are usually arranged in flat-topped groups called umbels, where the flower stalks seem to grow from a common point.

Right: Red columbine from the Rocky Mountains of North America. The flower has five red sepals and five pink petals, each with a long, hollow, backward-pointing spur at its base. The nectar concealed in these spurs is only available to insects with long mouth parts.

Below: A wind-pollinated castor oil plant in tropical Africa. The bright red styles of the female flowers are in the upper part of the inflorescence, with the yellow anthers of the male flowers below. These anthers illustrate a rare phenomenon: they actively eject pollen into the atmosphere. Most other plants simply let the pollen fall out when the anther walls break down.

Willow catkins are clusters of all male or all female flowers. In this male pussy willow catkin the most conspicuous colour is provided by the pollen in the anthers. Willows are pollinated by insects and produce copious nectar but they have many of the characteristics of wind-pollinated flowers and like many other plants may transfer pollen by both means.

47

Left: Fuchsias are native to south and central America, though they are now widely grown elsewhere. In this species there is a very effective colour contrast between sepals and petals, enhancing the attraction of the colours to pollinators.

The New World orchids in the genus *Masdevallia* are typically some shade of purplish red. Like many flowers of this colour they are probably pollinated by flies. The almost fluorescent shine on this species makes it even more attractive.

In a large number of flowers the petals and sepals look the same and in these the outer floral parts are referred to collectively as the perianth. Well known examples are lilies, tulips and hyacinths. Both sepals and petals tend to be much smaller, even absent altogether, in plants that use wind and water for pollination and which therefore have no need for any visually attractive parts.

After the petals have completed a period of attraction and, in the normal course of events, pollination has taken place, they wither and fall away from the flower. They are therefore at their most brilliant and colourful when the flower is mature. Some petals actually change colour as they age. This may increase the attraction of the clustered flowers since the colour changes may be bright and contrasting like the reds and yellows of the red-hot poker and the reds and blues of viper's bugloss. In other species the colour changes have a different and sometimes unknown function. This is the case with the flowers of the giant water lily *Victoria amazonica:* these change from white to purplish red during the single day in which they mature. Similarly morning glory petals can be blue in the morning and pink in the afternoon. It is likely that in some cases the colour change may signal to the pollinator that the flower is fertilized and no longer producing nectar. This could be very advantageous since the animal saves time and energy by not visiting

The flower of the gloriosa lily changes colour from yellow to pink after fertilization. This may be a signal that the flower has been pollinated and is therefore no longer producing nectar.

Right: As the flowers of red hot pokers mature they change from red to yellow. It is not known if the red carotenoid pigments are converted to yellow or if yellow pigments are always there but are unmasked when the red disappears. Flowers of all ages occur on the inflorescence, the young ones giving the red tip. The colour contrast makes them more attractive to the sunbirds that pollinate them in the wild.

foodless flowers and from the plant's point of view the pollen is being used most efficiently.

Some petals have an additional appendage called a corona to make them look even more attractive to their pollinators. The trumpets of daffodils and narcissi are coronas. The yellow corona of forget-me-nots against the blue of the petals makes the flowers look like bright little eyes and gives them their old country names of 'robin's eye' and 'bird's eye'. In some milkweeds, too, the yellow corona forms an attractive contrast with the petals. Passion flowers are a large and particularly spectacular group of corona-bearing plants. Some, including the widely cultivated giant granadilla have a banded fringe forming a large corona which is the most attractive part to pollinators. Others like purple granadilla use contrasting colours of corona and petals. Most of this large genus come from South America and are grown both for their unique flowers and for their juice and fruit. Their name was given by early Spanish friars who saw symbols of Christ's passion in the flowers.

There are also other, less spectacular ways in which petals are coloured. Some lines and blobs form guides to direct insects to the nectar. These will be discussed in

Two species of passion flower (right and below) illustrate the group's variety. The 'fringe' is a corona, which often contrasts in colour with the petals. Passion flowers were named by early Spanish missionaries to South America who saw the symbols of Christ's passion in the strange form of the flowers. The five anthers represent the five wounds Christ received on the cross, the triple style is the three nails and the central receptacle is the pillar of the cross. The corona forms the crown of thorns and the five sepals and petals together represent the ten apostles (excluding Peter and Judas). The calyx is the halo around Christ's head. *Passiflora incarnata* (right) is mainly pollinated by large carpenter bees, which are attracted by its ultra violet or 'bee purple' colour and can span the space between its nectaries and anthers. Smaller insects may steal the nectar without pollinating. The red cultivated species (below) is especially attractive to hummingbirds.

more detail in the next chapter. A special case of petal colour contrast occurs in many members of the Compositae – a huge family which includes many garden plants. In these the 'flower' is really a composite head (hence the family name) of lots of tiny flowers called florets. In many, the outer florets have one petal expanded into a ray which contrasts with the small-petalled flowers in the central or tube florets. The daisy, for example, has white ray florets around the outside and yellow tube florets in the centre while *Rudbeckia bicolor*, one of the coneflowers from North America that has become a popular garden annual, has yellow ray florets and black central tube florets. In flowers such as dandelions and double chrysanthemums and dahlias there are only ray florets with no tube florets for contrast. Conversely, the common garden weed groundsel has only tube florets with no contrasting rays.

In upward-facing flowers, especially those with spreading petals and sepals, the inside surface of the petals is the brightest part. When flowers are naturally inverted or 'nodding', like the fritillary, the outside tends to be more conspicuously coloured than the inside.

As well as attracting animals, petals also provide them

The intensely dark centre of this African mallow acts like a bull's eye on a target, guiding insects to the stamens and styles where they can find nectar and pollination can take place.

Right: The drooping flowers of the fritillary have their most vivid colouring on the outside. Flowers which grow in the commoner upright position expose their inner surface, usually the brighter part.

with an alighting place. Many of the legumes – broom, sweet peas and lupins for example – have two petals which form a kind of handhold while two below interlock to make the keel. The fertile parts of the flower are enclosed within the keel, sometimes held back like a coiled spring. As the insect lands, its weight presses the keel down and releases the stamens and stigma which strike the underside of the pollinator. Pollen already clinging to the insect is deposited on the stigma while new pollen brushes on to it from the stamens. In many legumes the different parts of the flower are of contrasting colours.

The sepals and petals or perianth form the outer parts of the flower and take no direct part in the process of seed production. They are known as the sterile whorls. The inner fertile whorls, the stamens which produce the pollen grains and the innermost carpels which contain the ovaries, are also sometimes involved in attracting pollinators.

The stamens of most flowers consist of a stalk called a filament which supports the anther, a box-like container for the pollen grains. They sometimes take the place of petals as the main attractive organ of the flower. The most conspicuous part of gum-tree flowers is the brush of long stamens that are revealed when the petals fall away. Since gum-tree flower petals fall before the

Some willow herbs do not rely solely on their petals to signal to pollinators. Here the four-lobed, cross-shaped stigma forms an important component of the flower's visual attraction.

Left: Sweet pea flowers have a structure typical of many legumes. The large, upper petal is flanked by two side petals called wings. Below, two petals interlock to form a keel. This arrangement is a special adaptation to bee pollination.

The blossoms of *Acacia* (right) and *Eucalyptus* trees (below) have numerous stamens which dominate the flower heads, making them look like balls or brushes. The mass of colourful filaments is the visually attractive part of the flower. In many *Acacias* the stamens from several flowers are clustered together in a brilliant mass of yellow.

flower itself is fully mature, it is left to the tuft of stamens to attract insect pollinators to their plentiful supply of nectar. Many *Eucalyptus* have predominantly whitish or yellowish tufts of stamens but some, such as the scarlet flowering gum, are brilliant red with golden tips of pollen. The bottlebrush trees, close relatives of *Eucalyptus* and also originating in Australia, have conspicuous bright scarlet stamens, forming cylindrical spikes near the ends of their branches. A member of the pea family *Calliandra surinamensis* has very showy stamens which are white at the base and pink at the top. Many acacias have brilliant yellow blooms with the stamens from twenty to thirty flowers clustered together, their tiny

Herb paris is a woodland herb of Europe and western Asia. The dark purple ovary is the most colourful part of its flower and contrasts well with the pale yellow anthers. The perianth parts are green and relatively inconspicuous.

Poinsettias are probably the most widely known of the huge genus *Euphorbia*. The bright red parts are modified leaves which surround the flower clusters and act as the attracting part to pollinators. The yellow colour of the central clusters comes from bracts surrounding the tiny flowers.

Bougainvillea is a much cultivated ornamental plant. The flowers, growing in small groups, attract night-flying moths and the purple bracts around them draw pollinators' attention during the day.

A flamingo flower from tropical America. The green 'tail' is an inflorescence or spadix made up of many individually inconspicuous flowers. The red surround is a spathe which attracts pollinators.

more conspicuous than the tiny flowers they surround. Similarly the most colourful part of the popular Christmas poinsettia is the beautiful deep red of its modified foliage leaves. These substitute petals draw the attention of insects to the clusters of tiny flowers. Another form of bract is called a spathe and is a sort of hood surrounding a long cylindrical cluster of tightly massed simple flowers – the spadix. Spathes and spadices are found in the Arum family. Many, though not all spathes are bright and attractive to pollinators; the flamingo flower gives a bright red splash of colour in the rain forest of Central America while the South African pink calla has a spathe of beautifully delicate pink. The water arum has a white spathe as does the calla or arum lily, surely the best known of them all. This majestic plant has become very popular with florists for its arrow-shaped leaves as well as for its flower head. It comes from the coastal and montane parts of South Africa where it is more appreciated for its starchy rhizomes which are dug up and fed to pigs. It has become naturalized in Australia and there it has sunk even lower as it has become an agricultural weed.

The colourful effect of flowers is often increased by massing them together in bunches of various shapes. The umbel is a common shape and characteristic of the family Umbelliferae, a family which includes many plants of European roadsides. When flowers are massed together on one plant, they must also mature simultaneously for maximum effect – a rather difficult achievement. Sometimes the outer flowers of heads, umbels or similar masses of flowers are larger than the inner ones. These larger flowers often act only as an attractive signal for they may have imperfectly developed stamens and carpels which make them sterile. The guelder rose is one of these, with a ring of large sterile white flowers surrounding the smaller, relatively inconspicuous but fertile blooms.

Pollinating indoor plants

Special pollination problems occur in horticultural plants grown indoors where the plant's natural colour signals to animals may be frustrated. The tomato, although self-pollinated, needs to be disturbed if pollen transfer is to be ensured. Gardeners frequently tap the stakes supporting the plants to shake the flowers at the right time while commercial growers have developed electrical vibrators to do the job for them. For plants which need to have pollen moved from one individual to another, gardeners must use a paintbrush to do the insect's job of picking up pollen and placing it on the stigma of another plant.

sepals and petals still at their bases. In all these examples it is the stem-like filament of the stamen that is conspicuous, but there are flowers where the anther, or the pollen that it encloses provide the dominant colour. Male willow catkins, for example, have bright yellow anthers which are probably the main visual signal to pollinating insects.

The carpels in the centre of the flower vary greatly in size, shape, number and the degree to which they are fused together. They consist of the ovary, usually surmounted by a stalk called a style and capped by the stigma. They rarely play a major part in attracting insects but in herb paris, the dark violet ovary makes a striking contrast with the bright yellow stamens which encircle it. In some willow-herbs the stigmas form a white cross which contrasts with the pink of their petals.

Occasionally coloured parts outside the flowers are used to add to or provide the entire colour signal to animals. Bougainvillea has colourful bracts which are

Colours that attract insects

Insect vision

It is very difficult for a human being to imagine the visual world of insects. Their eyes are quite different from ours in structure and function and thus give a totally different view of the surrounding world. Insects have compound eyes built from many simple elements called ommatidia which appear as tiny facets when we see them in surface view. It is believed that they are particularly good at detecting movement but since the focus cannot be altered, flower-visiting insects probably have less sharp vision than we do. Nevertheless, many experiments have shown that insects are attracted by the bright colours of flowers from considerable distances and may also be guided around the flower surface by small marks or guidelines at a range of no more than a few millimetres.

In many insect-pollinated flowers the attractions provided by the colours are reinforced by scents but the relative importance of the two varies considerably. Some flowers use scent for guiding insects from a distance while others use it only close to. In other cases the scents merely stimulate the insects to search for food and still other plants do not use scents at all. Sometimes insects can be prevented from visiting plants if the flowers are given an unaccustomed scent.

The most detailed studies of vision in insects have been carried out on bumble and honey bees but the conclusions seem to apply to many other groups. First of all the experimenters had to find out whether insects can distinguish colours. A scientist, Karl von Frisch, did this by using coloured pieces of paper as markers to attract honey bees to a bowl of sugared water, a favourite food. First he trained them to feed at sugar-water placed on blue paper and discovered that they would soon go to blue paper even if there was no food on it. If the bees were given a choice of grey or blue they still flew to the

Anthurium lily from Cape Province, South Africa. These striking lilies are common roadside plants. Bees, which are attracted to them in large numbers, are the main pollinating agents. The white 'hood' is a spathe, surrounding the tightly massed flowers of the spadix.

The hogweed has flowers with easily
accessible nectar. Accordingly they are
visited by a range of unspecialized, short-
tongued insects which are able to feed at the
nectaries. More specialized long-tongued
insects may also occasionally feed there.

blue, showing that they were responding to the colour
and not just to a difference in the brightness of light
reflected from the pieces of paper. Further training
showed that the bees could detect six different colours:
ultra-violet, bluish-green, violet, 'bee purple', yellow
and blue. In other words their vision is shifted along the
light spectrum from ours towards the shorter wavelengths of light.

Bees are extremely sensitive to ultra-violet light, which
is completely invisible to man. We saw in Chapter 1
how light made up of all the colours of our visible spectrum appears white to us. The corresponding colour for
bees has a component of ultra-violet light and lacks red.
A flower that reflects all light including ultra-violet
would still appear white to us but would be a different
'bee white' to bees. In practice 'bee white' flowers are
rare but the different visual spectrum of bees has an
effect on other colours, too. For example, it is well
known that purple colour can be produced by mixing
the colours at the opposite ends of our visual spectrum
i.e. red and blue. A corresponding 'bee purple' is made
by mixing the colours yellow and ultra-violet which are

at opposite ends of the bee's spectrum. The ultra-violet
component means that the bees see many colours incon-
ceivable to us. Bees are so sensitive to ultra-violet light
that they can detect yellow light with a mere 2% ultra-
violet light as a distinct colour from plain yellow. By
contrast they are much less sensitive to yellow light. The
yellow component in an ultra-violet/yellow mixture had
to reach 50% before bees could distinguish the colour
from pure ultra-violet.

There is no doubt that there are many flowers which
will look quite different to man and insects and by using
special filters and photographic methods it is possible to
discover more about the colours insects see. The flowers
of the wild cherry appear white to us because they reflect
all the colours of our visible spectrum – blue, green, red
etc. Since bees cannot see the red colour the flowers to
them will appear blue-green – white light without the
red component. The purple flowers of heather, which reflect a mixture of red and blue light, will appear blue to
bees. The flowers of creeping cinquefoil are yellow to us
but reflect also an invisible ultra-violet component. To
bees they must appear 'bee purple', a mixture of yellow

The hoverfly's large, compound eyes curve round its head giving a broad field of vision. Hoverflies are attracted to the bright colours of flowers from a considerable distance. They feed on both nectar and pollen and most visit flowers where nectar is easy to extract.

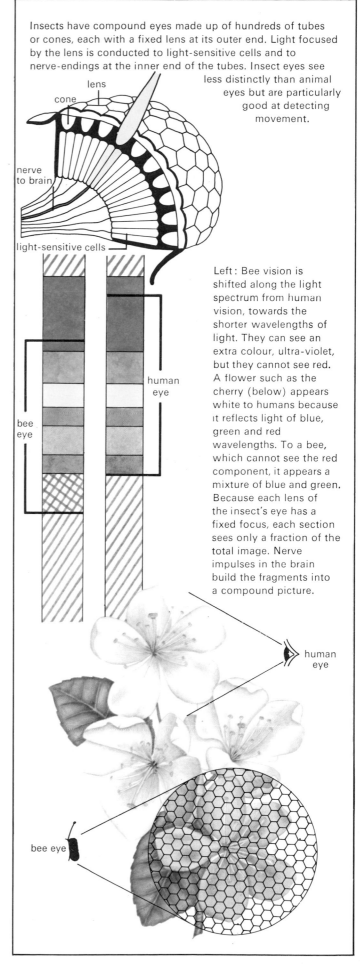

Insects have compound eyes made up of hundreds of tubes or cones, each with a fixed lens at its outer end. Light focused by the lens is conducted to light-sensitive cells and to nerve-endings at the inner end of the tubes. Insect eyes see less distinctly than animal eyes but are particularly good at detecting movement.

Left: Bee vision is shifted along the light spectrum from human vision, towards the shorter wavelengths of light. They can see an extra colour, ultra-violet, but they cannot see red. A flower such as the cherry (below) appears white to humans because it reflects light of blue, green and red wavelengths. To a bee, which cannot see the red component, it appears a mixture of blue and green. Because each lens of the insect's eye has a fixed focus, each section sees only a fraction of the total image. Nerve impulses in the brain build the fragments into a compound picture.

and ultra-violet. As a final example, the corn poppy is one of only a few truly red flowers found in Europe. Ironically, its splendid red must go unappreciated by bees and the reasons for the development of the colour remain a mystery. To a bee the petals will be the colour of ultra-violet, since they reflect this light, and the flower will have a black centre since the stamens are 'bee black'.

Work on the vision of other groups of pollinating insects has not been as intensive as that carried out on bees but we know that all the higher flies (Diptera) and butterflies and moths (Lepidoptera) can distinguish colours. It appears that many insects are red blind but sensitive to ultra-violet like bees. There are many exceptions to this, however, and red vision is known to occur in some butterflies for example.

Pollination by flies

Many flies are important pollinating animals. Most do not possess long mouth parts and can obtain nectar only from flowers which are flat, slightly concave or have a shape that makes the nectar easy to reach. In general flies visit flowers more for nectar than pollen though there are several species which appreciate pollen as an important part of their diet. Though they may visit the flowers only to take nectar, they are, of course, effective pollinators.

The flowers where nectar is easily accessible are often white, pink, yellow or green and unspecialized flies show a preference for these colours. The flowers of ivy, hogweed, golden saxifrage, sycamore, buttercups and hawthorn are all fly-pollinated. Flies do visit purple and blue flowers but since these frequently conceal their nectar it is only flies with more specialized feeding adaptations that take the food. As always, the true situation is rather more complex since these specialized flies also visit the simpler flowers while the more complex flowers are not always purple and blue. Hoverflies are one of the specialized species that have a long tongue and can reach concealed nectar. They get their name from their habit of remaining practically stationary in the air. They feed from such flowers as the germander speedwell (blue), thistles (purple) and bluebells (blue).

Amongst the most specialized flower feeders are the 'bee flies', so-called because they resemble bumble bees. Some of these have mouth parts over 10 mm long and so can pollinate flowers with quite deeply concealed nectar such as dog violets, bugles, cowslips and primroses.

It is often said that flies are attracted to small glistening objects, and it has been proved that greenbottle flies, blowflies, and flesh-flies all head for glistening droplets as soon as they hatch out. In grass of parnassus the tips of sterile stamens form small, glistening knobs which apparently attract flies to them. This is carried a stage further in *Tavaresia*, one of the milkweed family. *Tavaresia* has a bell-shaped, translucent corolla surrounding ten filaments, each ending in a little dark red knob. The knobs hang down, constantly vibrating in a breeze and can be seen through the corolla. Other plants have fine hairs which produce strange shimmering effects when they move in air currents and these are believed to be particularly attractive to flies.

A number of flowers attract flies by imitating the colour and smell of rotting flesh. These flowers are often dull brown, purple, yellow or spotted and generally mimic carrion, festering wounds or rotting meat. Greenbottle flies and blowflies normally prefer yellow and orange colours, and apparently choose brown, purple-brown or black flowers only if there is also a smell of faeces or decomposing matter. The intensity of colour and smell increases towards the centre of the flower, attracting the flies to the fertile parts where pollination can take place. The succulent carrion flowers of Africa and southern Asia have flowers of this sort and are so

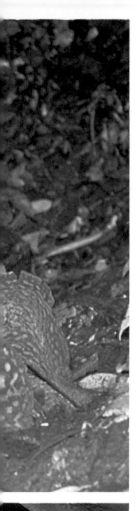

Rafflesia is a tropical parasitic flowering plant with no chlorophyll. This species, *R. arnoldii*, has the largest flowers in the world. They are coloured and smell like carrion and this attracts flies to pollinate them.

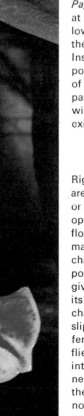

Left: The colours and waxy sheen on this *Paphiopedilum* orchid lure flies into holes at the base of the pouch formed by the lower petal. The flies cannot escape through the holes because the inside is slippery. Instead they are forced to travel through the pouch along a route provided with footholds of long hairs. During this short journey they pass the stigma and anthers and are dusted with pollen. They are released through an exit hole (not visible).

Right: The flowers of the cuckoo pint are at the base of the plant's central column or spadix. The lower part of the spathe (cut open here) forms a chamber round the flowers; the lowest ring are females with the males above them. At the top of the chamber is a ring of stiff, downward-pointing hairs. The exposed part of the spadix gives off a putrid smell which attracts flies to its slippery surface. The flies fall to the chamber below and are trapped by the slippery walls and the ring of hairs. The female flowers are mature at this stage so flies carrying pollen from other plants come into contact with and fertilize them. The next day the hairs shrivel and the walls lose their slipperiness so the flies can escape. By now the male flowers are mature and producing pollen, which dusts the flies as they leave, preparing them for fertilizing the female flowers of the next plant which traps them.

convincing that the female flies lay eggs in them. When the larvae hatch, no food is available, so they are doomed to starve.

The fantastic fly-pollinated flowers of parasitic *Rafflesia* species are found in the South-east Asian rain forests. The rare *Rafflesia arnoldii* is known the world over because it has the largest of all flowers, some growing to a metre across and weighing up to 9 kg. The stinking flowers have structures similar to petals and sepals but in other ways are very unusual. Although fourteen species of the genus *Rafflesia* have been described, all from Malaya and the East Indies, they have been studied so slightly that we know very little about their structure. It has been claimed that some local tribesmen know more about *Rafflesia* than botanists, since they collect the flower buds to make into invigorating love potions!

Some plants actually trap pollinating flies, forcing them to come into contact with the stigmas and anthers. In these, colour still plays an important part, as the fly must be lured to the plant before the trap can operate. In the tropical genus *Ceropegia*, the lengthened tube of fused petals forms a trap of delicate greens, greys and browns in which the flies are imprisoned. The lantern-

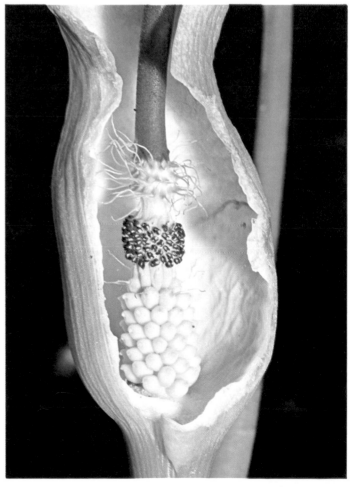

like shape of the flower seems particularly attractive to flies.

The pelican flower, a climbing plant from Central America has a tubular flower with a large conspicuous lobe, some 12 cms wide and 20 cms long. The lobe is yellowish in colour with a chequered pattern of reddish veins and, when ready for pollination, smells of rotting fish. The tubular flower is U-shaped with one end closed. At the closed end of the U are the stigmas and anthers and surrounding them there are translucent cells which give an effect called a 'window pane'. Flies are attracted to the colourful lobe at the open end of the U and fall down the tube. Inside, downward-pointing hairs prevent them from climbing out again. On the other side of the bend the U has hairs which enable the fly to move upwards where it is attracted to the light of the window pane and hence to the stigmas and anthers. The flies are released eventually when the trapping hairs shrivel and the tube entrance widens. They are then free to be trapped again by another flower so that pollination can be completed. The window panes (which are found in several other fly-trapping plants) are hardly a plant colour but are certainly an ingenious use of light by plants.

Some fly-trapping plants use a patch of brightness to attract insects to them initially. *Arisaema laminatum* (a member of the Arum family) has tiny flowers that cluster together into a central column, the spadix, surrounded by a distinctive bract or spathe. The lower half of the purple spathe forms a tube round the spadix whilst the upper half opens out into a hood. The tissue of the spathe has translucent panels which refract and reflect light to give a concentration of brightness at the entrance to its tubular part. The contrasting dark colours of its hood make the bright area even more effective.

Orchids provide examples of some of the most ingenious fly-trapping flowers. The wax-lustred flowers of the slipper orchids are pollinated by forcing flies into a trap and ensuring that they brush against the fertile parts of the flowers as they leave. The upper sepal is often striped – possibly to give a light focusing effect. These orchids are usually green, brown, dull red, purple and white in various combinations and, as is so typical in fly-pollinated flowers, there is often a bad smell.

Pollination by beetles

A number of flowers are pollinated either solely or chiefly by beetles. They are usually either large single flowers like magnolias and water lilies or small, clustered flower heads such as dogwood and elder.

Since beetles generally have poor eyesight but a good

Flowers adapted for pollination by beetles tend to be white or pale coloured since beetles have poor eyesight. Many beetles feed on the soft parts of the flower and do considerable damage. The flower's ovules are therefore usually hidden away from the insect's jaws. The plant here is an Australian flowering shrub *Ricinocarpus glaucus*.

Buddleia is especially attractive to butterflies, even in countries to which it is not native. Butterflies such as this peacock gather at the flowers to feed on their nectar and so pollinate them.

A brimstone butterfly feeds on a thistle flower. Flowers which hide their nectar in elongated floral tubes are often purple or blue and can be successfully pollinated only by insects with long, sucking mouth parts.

sense of smell the flowers they pollinate tend to be of white or dull colours with strong odours. The smells are usually fruity or as though something is fermenting and are quite unlike the sweet and attractive odours of flowers pollinated by butterflies, moths and to a lesser extent, bees.

Some beetle-pollinated flowers secrete nectar but beetles get most of their nourishment from such things as sap, fruit, leaves, dung and carrion. Many beetles chew directly at the petals of the flowers they are visiting or eat special food bodies or pollen. For safety, beetle-pollinated flowers usually have their ovules hidden well out of reach of the chewing jaws.

Pollination by butterflies and moths

The order Lepidoptera includes many important flower pollinators which are guided by a combination of sight and smell. The flowers they visit tend to have a nectary at the base of a slender, tubular corolla or a long spur. Most butterflies and moths have long, sucking mouth parts and there is a close link between the length of their tongue and the length of the corolla tube or spur of the flowers they visit. Tongues can vary from a few millimetres in length in small moths to 1 to 2 cms in many butterflies, 2 to 8 cms in some hawkmoths of northern

temperate regions and up to an incredible 25 cms in some tropical moths.

Butterflies are mainly active during the day. In Britain the native flowers most adapted structurally to pollination by butterflies are often blue, like forget-me-nots or deep pink like pinks, pyramidal orchids and fragrant orchids. In southern Europe there are some red butterfly-pollinated flowers such as Maltese cross and many tropical and subtropical plants pollinated by butterflies have scarlet flowers. The relatively frequent occurrence of red flowers pollinated by butterflies seems to confirm that many butterflies, unlike bees, can see red. Flowers of many other colours are also pollinated by butterflies, especially where they are tubular and are grouped in compact heads like golden rod and white yarrow.

A hundred years ago, a scientist called Hermann Müller observed butterflies in the Alps and claimed that they preferred flowers of similar colours to themselves. He thought the colour preference used in choosing a mate must have become transferred to the choice of flowers. The great naturalist H. W. Bates reported a similar phenomenon in the Amazonian rain forest. Unfortunately there has been little work done recently to confirm or refute this attractive hypothesis.

It has been found that butterflies which feed exclu-

Yucca moths and yucca flowers are interdependent. After collecting pollen from the centre of one flower, the female moth stores it in a small lump under her head. She then flies to another flower and, if the ovary is ripe, bores a hole into it and lays an egg. In this picture, the moth has layed her egg and then climbed up to the stigmas to place pollen on them. This ensures that they are fertilized. The seeds that develop provide food for the growing moth larvae. Yuccas have been introduced in the West Indian islands and in the Old World, but, without their moth partners, they produce no seeds.

sively on flowers may have an instinctive colour response. In experiments with flower models one group of butterflies, including the small tortoiseshell and large tortoiseshell preferred yellow and blue colours whilst another group, including large white and brimstone preferred blue, violet and purple. This seems to agree with published field observations on the colours of flowers these species prefer.

Some flowers visited during the day by butterflies are visited at night by moths. Many flowers are, however, exclusively pollinated by moths and these show several distinct features. The hummingbird hawkmoth is exceptional in that it flies by day and visits flowers which are also favoured by butterflies, but most species of moth are nocturnal and flowers adapted to visits by them are often white, pale rose or pale yellow. Many also have a strong fragrance which they send out after sunset to help guide the moth from a distance. The large, white flowers of the moth-pollinated tobacco plant are well known for their heavy, sweet scent.

Good examples of moth-pollinated flowers are the night-scented catchfly and the Nottingham catchfly where the flowers are inconspicuous during the day. The petals of the night-scented catchfly are rosy inside and yellow outside and curl up during the day, reopening at night when the flower becomes fragrant. The Nottingham catchfly also rolls up its petals during the day and is

particularly notable for the way it passes through three different stages on three successive nights. On the first night the petals are horizontal and the first whorl of stamens are mature. On the second night the petals are drawn back and a second set of stamens replaces the first set. On the third night these too wilt and the mature style protrudes. Through all three nights the flower remains fragrant and attractive to night-flying moths.

It is interesting to note the differences between members of the same genus when one species adapts itself for diurnal and another for nocturnal pollination. Two campions commonly found in European hedgerows illustrate this point well as the crimson petals of the red campion make it conspicuous during the day while the

white campion opens its white flowers in the evening, when it also becomes fragrant. Although these plants are very similar and might even occur in the same hedgerow the red campion is usually visited by insects active during the day. As dusk falls the white campion will appear very striking while its red relative will blend into the dark background and go unnoticed by nocturnal insects.

As we have suggested, some moths favour flowers with long tubular corollas or spurs. Particularly fine examples of this type of flower are the butterfly orchid (which is named from the shape of its flowers, not the insects which pollinate it) and the honeysuckles. Moths swarm around these species during the evenings, carrying pollen from one flower to another. The abundant supply of nectar in some honeysuckle species makes them particularly attractive to robber insects and, indeed, to children who catch drops of the nectar as they pull off the corolla tubes. Very few pollinators are dependent on a particular plant species. The yucca moths and yucca plants, however, are involved in a highly specialized relationship which benefits them both. The female moth scrapes pollen from the creamy white, heavily scented flowers at night and rolls it into a ball. Her mouth is specially adapted and she is able to carry the pollen ball to another yucca flower. Here she pierces the flower's ovary wall and lays her eggs among the ovules. She then packs the ball of pollen through the opening of the stigma so ensuring that pollination takes place and the yucca seeds develop. So, too, do the larvae of the moth and as they grow they feed on the yucca seeds. When fully grown the larvae gnaw their way through the ovary wall and make their way to the ground. The moths benefit because their larvae have a safe and nourishing home. The plant benefits because it is certain of pollination and as the larvae eat only about 20% of the developing seeds, there are always plenty available to produce new yuccas. Such close relationships between pollinators and flowers are rare. The only comparable example is that between figs and fig-wasps.

Because moth-pollinated flowers tend to be pale coloured it is surprising to find that not only do moths have extremely good eyesight in poor light but they also have good colour vision.

Pollination by ants, wasps and bees

Only a few plants are ant-pollinated. Ants are hairless so that pollen does not stick to them, they lack special pollen-collecting devices and are unable to move rapidly

Queen of the night, or night-blooming cereus grows wild in the West Indies, but was introduced as a garden flower in Europe around 1700. Its delicate white petals open at night to attract night-flying insects. By the next day, the flower is withered.

from plant to plant. In temperate regions ant-pollinated flowers are likely to be small, green and inconspicuous and the ants must be attracted by scent rather than by any special colour. In tropical regions they may be more important: ants have been reported to pollinate the economically important cocoa and possibly cashew and lychee as well.

Many plants have developed adaptations to prevent ants visiting the flowers and robbing them of nectar and pollen. Some have developed impassable barriers like the sticky stem of the red German catchfly. The teasel protects its flowers by a series of 'moats' at the base of its leaves. Others decoy ants by producing nectaries away from the flowers, like those on the leaves of some vetches. The ants are able to feed on the nectar without disturbing the pollen. True pollinators, however, are rewarded with nectar produced within the flowers.

The wasps of the family Vespidae, which includes the species recognized as 'wasps' by most people, are known to pollinate several species of plant. They seem to prefer small pinkish or dark brownish-red flowers but since wasps are known to be blind to red light, flowers of this colour must appear very dark to them. Amongst flowers especially favoured by wasps are figworts, the orchid helleborines, cotoneasters with brownish-red flowers and the snowberry.

Of all the hymenopterans the bees are by far the most important as pollinators. This is not surprising when you consider that there are 20,000 known species, nearly all of which visit flowers for food. They are abundant in many parts of the world and in both larval and adult stages of their life cycle they are dependent on flowers. The adults feed on nectar, sometimes supplemented by pollen. The larvae, too, are fed on nectar (converted to honey) and pollen both of which are collected by the female adult bees.

It is rather difficult to pick out any colours characteristic of bee-pollinated flowers since bees visit such a wide range of species. Between them all the different species of bees will visit almost any flower that is available, although their choice may be somewhat restricted at certain seasons. However, for substantial lengths of time the worker bees are, on the whole, constant to particular species of flowers. This constancy makes them very efficient pollinators and means that they can also influence the plants' evolution: those that are best adapted to the bees' needs will be pollinated most regularly and will therefore produce most seeds.

Bee-pollinated flowers characteristically are showy and bright. Their nectaries are at the base of corolla tubes so that only insects with specially adapted mouth parts

Common wasp feeding on and pollinating a broad-leaved helleborine; a mass of pollen sticks to the wasp's head as it probes for nectar inside the flower.

can reach them and they frequently have landing platforms to support the bee while it feeds or gathers food. Among many flowers pollinated by bees are coltsfoot, primroses and cowslips and many Composites such as tansy and hawkweeds. Several members of the pea family, which includes flowers such as gorse, broom and clover are among those with structural adaptations to bees.

Purple loosestrife is a particularly interesting bee-pollinated species as it has an elaborate system associated with its cross-pollination. The plants have three distinct types of flower with different lengths of style and stamens. One type has a short style coupled with either long or medium length stamens, another has a medium length style with either short or long stamens and the final type has a long style and either short or medium

Honeybees produce honey as food for their larvae. Special behavioural adaptations enable them to signal to one another where suitable flowers are, and they also tend to develop a constancy for visiting particular species of plant.

Above, left: A bumble bee probes for nectar in the florets of a composite flower. The pollen basket on its leg is clearly well filled.

Right: Many flowers have surface guide lines to provide a close range aid to alighting insects. The streaks on this foxglove flower probably help bees to find the nectar hidden at the base of the flower and thus bring them into contact with the anthers and stigma.

length stamens. Each type also has pollen grains of a different size and colour. Fully fertile seeds will usually develop only if the style which receives the pollen corresponds in length to the stamens from which the pollen was removed.

Many crop plants grown for their fruit or seeds are bee-pollinated. They include apples, pears, plums and cherries. A great deal of care has to be taken to ensure that bees are around at flowering times. Commercial orchards may cover large areas and when they are planted the natural habitat of native bees is often destroyed so that pollination problems can be acute. Sometimes honey bee hives are moved into the area and the bees may be trained to visit flowers to which they are unaccustomed. It is important to keep weed species out of cultivated areas. Plants such as dandelions with their showy yellow flowers could distract the bees from the tree blossom and cause a serious reduction in the amount of fruit that forms.

Floral guide marks

So far we have discussed the role of flower colours in attracting insects from a distance but colours also play a role in guiding the insect over the flower surface at close range. Many flowers possess guide marks, or lines on the petal surfaces, which may guide the insect to a nectar source or, in flowers without nectar, at least

ensure that the insect is in the correct position.

In 1922 Friedrich Knoll confirmed by means of some ingenious experiments that these marks serve to guide insects. To test the response of moths to colour patterns, he prepared papers with various dark violet markings on a light violet background. The papers were covered with glass plates and as Knoll fed the moths with syrup beforehand it was possible to see where they had probed with their mouthparts, since they left traces of syrup on the glass. Knoll concluded that nearly all the artificial guide marks had a direct effect and that circles were of major importance, acting like a 'bulls eye'.

There is no doubt that many insect-pollinated flowers have surface guide marks which reflect ultra-violet light and hence are invisible to us. An intensive survey was carried out on about two hundred bee-pollinated species by H. Kugler in the nineteen-sixties. He found that about 30% of the flowers investigated had patterns visible to humans and a further 26% had patterns in ultra-violet only. Many of the flowers with patterns visible to us also had additional ultra-violet patterns. In no case, though, was there any completely new design of patterning in ultra-violet. The abundance of these surface patterns makes it clear that they are of considerable importance in guiding insects at the flower surface to make sure that they touch the anthers and stigmas and complete pollination.

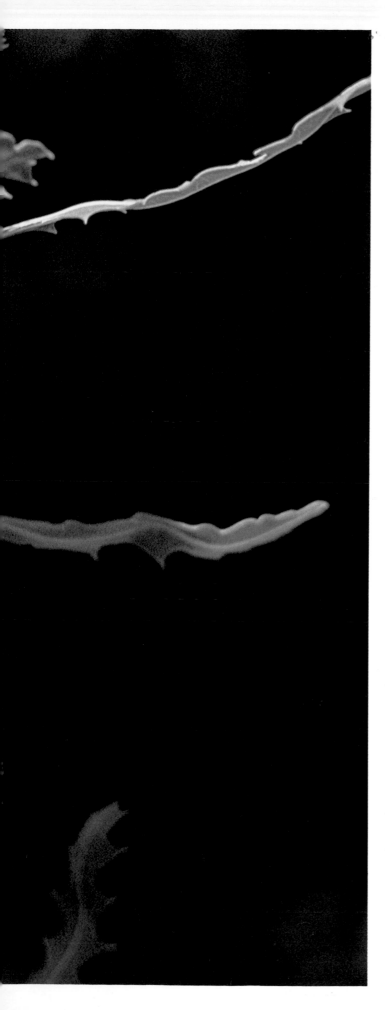

Colours that attract birds and bats

Pollination by birds

Pollination of flowers by birds is very important in many parts of the world although it is completely unknown in Europe and in Asia north of the Himalayas. Bird pollination does occur in temperate North America even as far north as Alaska but it is in the tropics that it is most common. Where it has evolved there is no doubt that birds are highly efficient pollinators and individual birds probably visit thousands of flowers in a day. Three families of birds are generally regarded as the main flower-visiting groups although over fifty other bird families are known to include pollinators.

The Americas are the only place in which the best known and most highly adapted bird pollinators of all, the hummingbirds, are found. Hummingbirds have thin bills, usually straight but sometimes curved down, and brush-tipped tongues to make collecting nectar easier. They have a special digestive system to cope with the large quantities of nectar they eat and a hovering flight which enables them to position themselves precisely in front of the flowers. There are over 300 species of hummingbird, many beautifully coloured. The largest is about 21 cm long with, at the other end of the scale, the bee hummingbird from Cuba which is little more than 5 cm long – and half of this is tail and bill!

Sunbirds (Nectarinidae) parallel hummingbirds in their adaptations and look superficially very like them but they are found in the tropics and subtropics of Africa, in South-east Asia and eastern Australia. They, too, have special tongues and a gut that enables nectar to bypass the gizzard and go straight to the intestine to speed up digestion. Sunbirds can hover but not as well as hummingbirds so they often perch on or near the flower.

The third important group of bird pollinators, the South African sugarbirds and Australasian honeyeaters

Grey-headed honeyeater on Ashby's banksia. The flowers, stem and leaves of this tall shrub, common on sandy heaths along the western Australian coast, provide firm perches for small birds. Pollen is transferred both on the bird's feet (when it perches on the flower) and on its beak as it probes deeply for nectar among the tightly packed flowers.

are classed together in the family Meliphagidae but they may not actually be closely related, and are probably only similar because they have adapted to visiting flowers in the same way. In some sugarbirds the tongue can be rolled into a tube for sucking up nectar.

Birds of other families which are locally important in pollination are the honeycreepers in Hawaii; brush-tongued lories and linkeets in eastern Australia; white-eyes in Africa, Asia and Australasia; flowerpeckers and parrots in Australasia and bulbuls and occasional members of the weavers, orioles and warblers in Africa. Many of these birds show no special structural adaptations to feeding at flowers and in fact almost all nectar-eating birds supplement their diet with insects. It is thought that insect-eating birds gradually evolved the habit of taking nectar, probably sipping it at first by chance whilst they were searching flowers for their staple insect food. Early stages in the process can perhaps be seen in birds like the garden warbler and willow warbler which are still mainly insectivorous.

The eyes of birds are constructed in a very similar way to our own. They see a similar range of colours but are particularly sensitive to the longer wavelengths of the visible spectrum. A consequence of this is that red and orange are more commonly found in bird-pollinated flowers than in those pollinated by other animals. Red or crimson, then orange and yellow are the most frequent colours with blue, violet, white and cream following in order of importance. A further reason for the abundance of reds in bird-pollinated flowers is that red flowers are less conspicuous to bees, which are thus not attracted to flowers they could not pollinate but might rob of nectar. Birds are not sensitive to ultra-violet light and this colour is not a feature of their flowers. Since birds have virtually no sense of smell the flowers they pollinate are typically unscented. One exception is the markedly scented bird-pollinated *Sejaria caracusana*.

The colours are often bright and vivid though some birds do feed at drab flowers such as *Buddleja brasiliensis*. The cardinal flower has such a spectacular, pure red spike of flowers that it has been a popular cultivated flower since 1626 when it was exported from its native North America to Europe. Scarlet sage and *Aloe excelsa* also attract their pollinators with brilliant scarlet flowers. *Tillandsia lindensiana* has equally spectacular flowers but here they are a beautiful cobalt blue.

Colour contrast may be as important as the colour itself and many authors have commented on the dramatic juxtaposition of different colours in bird-pollinated flowers. Red and yellow occur against a background of green while other frequent contrasts are blue and yellow,

The large size of this cultivated *Hibiscus* flower, its bright red colour and its shape are all part of its adaptation to bird pollinators. The flowers are at their best for only one day; after this the petals begin to wither.

New Holland honeyeater on a green kangaroo paw. The bird perches on the felted stems as it probes nearby flowers. In doing so, pollen is deposited on the bird's head and so transferred from flower to flower.

white and scarlet, and more rarely, black and yellow or black and scarlet. A multi-coloured bird-pollinated plant that is often grown by gardeners is *Bilbergia nutans*. It has a drooping flower head with pink or red bracts, a pink calyx, yellowish-green petals tipped with blue and protruding stamens with conspicuous yellow tips. Honeyeaters visit the State flower of Western Australia, kangaroo-paw, which has red stems and a green, tube-like flower with a red base. Other kangaroo-paws have contrasting colours: the Albany kangaroo-paw is green and red with an unusual grey interior while the black kangaroo-paw is actually black and green. Also from Australia are two bird-pollinated members of the pea family: bullock bush is red with a yellow centre and

Sturt's desert pea, perhaps the most handsome of all Australia's annuals, has red flowers with bulbous, velvet-black centres. The flowers of proteas also often provide good examples of contrasting colours, for instance the South African *Protea grandiceps*, with its scarlet, white-fringed bracts. Marks acting as close range signals to guide birds to the nectaries also give contrasting colours on the flower surface, but they are not generally as clear nor are they as common as they are on insect-pollinated plants.

We mentioned earlier that some butterflies may possibly prefer plants that are the same colour as they are themselves. A number of scientists have also noted that bird-pollinated flowers are often the same colour as the birds that visit them. The brilliant scarlet breast of the male sunbird *Cinnyris senegalensis*, for example, matches the bright *Aloe excelsa* that it pollinates. However, more research needs to be done on this subject before we know the purpose of the similarity.

Qne of the most common features of bird-pollinated flowers is that they have a copious supply of nectar. However, its sugar concentration may be as low as 5% and as the birds have a very high work rate, they must consume large quantities to supply them with the energy they need. A hummingbird, for instance, can consume up to half its body weight in sugar every day using its specially adapted gizzard to cope with the nectar. (In insect-pollinated flowers the sugar concentration is much higher, about 15%, and the weakness of bird-pollinated flowers' nectar may well help to exclude insects from competing there.) It has recently been shown that some Australian pollinating birds feed on pollen as well as nectar, and this habit may be more widespread than is usually thought.

Structural adaptations in bird-pollinated flowers

Bird flowers are often strongly constructed. Their ovaries may be protected from accidental pecks by surrounding tissue or they may be separated from the zone where nectar is secreted. Important exceptions, though, are the flowers visited by dainty hummingbirds, which may be as delicate as those pollinated by hawkmoths or butterflies.

The flowers most specialized to pollination by birds tend to fall into two groups. One type has long, slender corolla tubes which allow fine bills to be inserted and make sure that the bird's head is dusted with pollen while it is drinking the nectar. Aloes, red-hot pokers and South African heather all belong to this category and are visited by sunbirds and sugarbirds. Many New World hummingbird-pollinated flowers are of this shape as are also the *Clermontia* species of Hawaii. These plants have corolla tubes curved to match exactly the curve of the bills of the Hawaiian honeycreepers which feed at them.

The second main type consists of plants with brush-like flowers which dust their visitors with pollen more diffusely than the slender group. Australia, especially, has many flowers like this. In the myrtle family there are the *Eucalyptus*, *Beaufortia* and *Callistemon* species. *Callistemon* is Greek for 'beautiful stamen', but they are more often known by their less gracious common name of bottlebrushes. In the protea family *Banksia* species also have brush-like flower spikes which are sufficiently tough and wiry to withstand visits from relatively large birds such as the red wattle-bird.

Cuphea hookeriana, a bird-pollinated flower from the mountains of western Mexico. The red, tubular flowers attract long-beaked humming-birds to feed. The sticky hairs around them may be a device to prevent insects from stealing the nectar. Certainly this plant has captured several small flies.

Strelitzias are specifically adapted for pollination by birds and their nectar is effectively hidden from non-pollinating animals. Two of the petals enclose the anthers and stigma, while the third blocks the entrance to the nectaries. Sunbirds and sugarbirds perch on a special bract and as they reach for the nectar, their breast brushes against the stigma and presses on the two long petals. The bird's weight releases the anthers and its breast is brushed with pollen. Only when this has happened can the third petal, concealing the nectaries, be raised.

A few flowers have more specific adaptations, like those which develop special perches. The traveller's tree and bird of paradise flowers have rigid bracts conveniently positioned for their pollinating visitors. There are five species of bird of paradise flower, all native to South Africa, but they have become more widely cultivated because of their spectacular appearance. The flowers are enclosed in a horizontal boat-shaped sheath formed by the bracts and they emerge from this one by one every few days. Local people think of them as 'crane flowers', with the sharp bract looking like a bill, topped by a crest of yellow and purple flowers. The bright yellow parts of the crest are sepals, the purple parts are specially modified petals. Two of the petals form a purple spike enclosing the anthers and stigma and a third, smaller one blocks the entry to the nectaries. Sunbirds and sugarbirds perch on the bract and as they reach for the nectar, their breast brushes against the stigma and presses against the two longer petals. The pressure releases the anthers so that pollen is brushed onto the bird. It is only after the bird's weight has triggered this action that the third petal can be raised and the bird can reach its reward.

Another South African plant, *Antholyza ringens*, an iris, has a specially adapted branch on its flower shoot so that sunbirds can perch and lean over the flowers, dusting themselves and the stigmas with pollen. The generic name of this plant means 'flower in a rage', and refers to the two-lipped blooms which gape as if they are about to bite. It does not frighten off the birds, however.

The South American genus *Puya* is the tallest member of the bromeliads, with huge spikes of flowers, some reaching as high as 12m. In some species, the lower half of the spikes are crowded with flowers, whilst the upper half is sterile and provides a place for birds to perch and seek nectar. It is interesting that one species, *Puya venusta*, does not have bird perches and is visited only by hummingbirds, which can, of course, feed while hovering and do not need to land on the flower.

The adaptation of a plant to a bird pollinator is carried a stage further in flowers that will not open without the aid of a bird. Some of the African mistletoes are dependent on sunbirds in this way. Their flowers open when the sunbird puts its fine bill into a slit in the side of the corolla, which then bursts open so that the anthers spring out, scattering pollen onto the bird's feathers.

One of the sugarbirds (*Promerops cafer*) and protea shrubs are a remarkable example of co-evolution. The birds are almost completely dependent on the plants and will not leave areas where they grow unless there is a

Swamp bottlebrush, Western Australia. Many bird flowers attract their pollinators with the brightly coloured filaments of their stamens. As the birds probe for nectar (or occasionally pollen) their feathers are daubed with pollen, which is then carried to the next flower.

Right: The brilliant red waxy bracts of the oriental ginger are conspicuous to pollinators at a long distance. At close range pollinators, which probably include birds, are guided to the relatively small flowers by their contrasting white colour.

shortage of food. The plants normally provide food, both nectar and the insects that are attracted to them, a nest site among their branches and nest material from fluff from the flowers. They even provide baths after rain, when the birds perch on a stem and flap their wings against the leaves to send up a shower of water. The sugarbird breeds during the protea's flowering season and is then at its busiest, moving from flower to flower ensuring both that its young are well supplied with nectar and that pollination takes place. Sugarbirds take insects as well as nectar, but the fledglings take a larger proportion of nectar than adults.

In spite of all these special adaptations, many plants favoured by birds may also attract insect pollinators.

The long 'brushes' of this bottlebrush are formed from the stamens of hundreds of tiny flowers, massed together for greater effect.

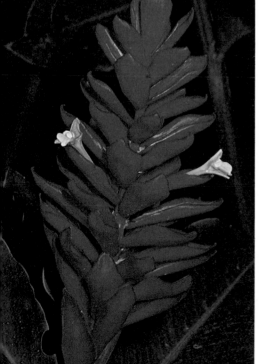

Below: This bat feeds almost exclusively on the pollen and nectar of the century plant *Agave palmeri*. Specially roughened hairs on the bat's head and neck are plastered with pollen from the massive exposed anthers.

The bat removes much of this with its long tongue, but enough remains to pollinate other flowers. In areas from which bats have been eliminated by humans, very few *Agave* plants are successfully pollinated.

The creeper *Cobaea scandens* from South America is one of the few cultivated ornamental plants that is pollinated by bats in its native country. The colour change of the bell-shaped flowers from white to dingy purple may signal to bats, even in poor light, that the flower has been pollinated and is no longer producing nectar.

Eucalyptus species, for instance, can be pollinated by flies and bees (including the honey bee, which was imported only quite recently into Australia) as well as by honeyeaters and parrots.

Pollination by bats

The pollination of flowers by bats, which are, of course, mammals, provides many interesting contrasts with bird pollination. Bat pollination is largely tropical and because it is difficult to make scientific observations, it has only recently been studied in detail. We now know that bats play an important role as pollinators. They are active mainly (but not entirely) in high trees or climbing plants and only at dusk or in the dark.

Bats belong to the order Chiroptera and pollinating species occur in both its suborders – Megachiroptera and Microchiroptera. Bats of the Megachiroptera are found in Africa, Asia and Australia and are divided into two groups, the fruit feeders and the nectar and pollen feeders. They are generally large and have relatively good eyesight but their echo-location system is not as good as that of the Microchiroptera. On the whole the fruit-

eating group are not pollinators while the bats that feed on nectar and pollen are. Pollen- and nectar-feeding bats include some of the smallest megachiropterans, only 5-6cms long.

The Microchiroptera feed mainly on insects but some tropical and sub-tropical American species are nectar feeders and pollinators. Research seems to suggest that they have evolved this habit more recently than the Old World bats.

All nectar-feeding bats have specially adapted mouth parts. Their tongues are long and slender, and have a brush of backward-pointing hairs at the tip. Bats usually alight to feed but some species have been seen hovering in front of night-blooming flowers, clinging to them for a moment as they insert their slender heads. As the bat thrusts in to reach the nectar it is daubed with pollen so that when it visits the next flower it pollinates it.

Bat-pollinated flowers have a number of characteristics in common. They tend to open only at night when the bats are active and, because bats fly in poor light, the flowers are never brightly coloured but are pale or even dark and dingy. Bats, unlike birds, have a very

The 15cm long, hanging baobab flower shows many of the characteristics of bat-pollinated species: it is pale in colour, strongly constructed, grows in an exposed position on the tree and has a brush of stamens to assist pollination.

Right: Honey possums are small marsupials specialized for a nectar and pollen diet. The flowers they feed on, such as this *Eucalyptus* species, are often adapted for pollination by birds. However, as the honey possum probes the blossoms for nectar, its head and body become dusted with pollen and this may well be transferred to the next flower it visits.

good sense of smell and they are helped to find the flowers by the strong scent the flowers give off, a smell rather like the smell of the bats themselves. The flowers of the African sausage tree smell like fermenting liquid.

The flowers are strongly constructed in order to bear the weight of the bat, and as many bats are quite clumsy fliers, needing plenty of room to manoeuvre, they are often placed well clear of other parts of the plant. They may dangle on long stalks like the flowers of the sausage tree and baobab or may be strategically placed close to the bare trunk or major branches of a tree, away from the foliage. The flowers produce large quantities of nectar and are often scored with claw marks which bear witness to the boisterous treatment given by the bats.

Flowers favoured by bats are usually either bell- or jaw-shaped, like the flowers of the sausage tree, or have brush- or ball-shaped blooms like the Asiatic *Giossampinus valetonii* and the durian. During the day, the dangling durian flowers, greenish yellow or pink remain closed and it is only after dusk that the petals curve back to reveal the brush of stamens. The baobab has a brush made up of conspicuous stamens which protrude

down beyond the corolla ring. The weird cries of bats visiting the baobab tree are thought to have helped give it its reputation for supernatural powers.

Parkia clappertonia, a member of the pea family from West Africa, has a more substantial, pollen-laden ball. Around the pendulous stalk the flowers are sterile but produce nectar, which collects in a shallow ring forming a trough round the top of the ball. As the bat clings to the ball and sips from the trough, its body is well dusted with pollen.

As *Parkia* flowers age they change from red to purple to salmon pink, a rather surprising colour change for a plant that is pollinated at night. A marked colour change also occurs in the violet ivy, one of the few bat-pollinated flowers that is popularly cultivated (in spite of its strong and rather unpleasant cabbagy smell). The flowers are green when they first open but as they age they gradually become purple and also lose their smell. They are visited and pollinated by birds as well as bats but the shape of the flowers (one of the bell-shaped group) and the frequent bat claw damage, suggest that bats are its most important pollinators.

Colours of fruits, seeds and spores

The last two chapters have dealt with the many devices plants use to make sure they are fertilized. A further range of plant mechanisms are needed to disperse the seeds and fruits that grow from the fertilized flower and in many of these colour plays a vital role. The dispersal mechanisms that have evolved are designed to move the seeds some distance so that when the young plant begins to grow, it is not competing with its parent for light, mineral nutrients or water in the soil. If a seed can be carried a long way, this may also enable the species to colonize new areas. The agents are the same ones that transport pollen – animals, wind and water, but there are, in addition, explosive mechanisms operated by the fruits themselves.

The production of seeds and fruits is the final role of the flower and once the egg cells have been fertilized, its sterile parts, which have assisted pollination, usually wither and drop off. The resources of the plant are channelled into the growth of the seeds and, usually, the surrounding wall of the ovary which develops into the fruit. The fruit both protects the seeds and provides them with a means of dispersal.

Fruits are usually divided into two main types, dry and fleshy. Dry fruits are like those of buttercups, sweet peas and poppies, which have a dry mature ovary wall. Fleshy fruits are like tomatoes, grapes and plums, with a juicy ovary wall. There is a further division into true and false fruits. True fruits (which include all those mentioned above) develop only from the ovary while false ones develop from other parts of the flower as well. Apples and pears are false fruits. Sometimes the ovaries of flowers are made up of many separate sections or carpels, each of which may develop into a separate fruit-let on the same fruit. The result is true fruits such as blackberries and raspberries. The strawberry is a false

These red Dartmouth apples are 'superfruits' compared with those which occur in the wild. However, if cultivated apples are allowed to ripen and fall they will still attract birds to feed on them. The seeds are eaten along with the fleshy parts but they are not digested, so may be deposited far from the parent tree, having passed through the bird's digestive system unharmed.

fruit: the swollen, red edible part comes not from the ovary wall but from the flower base, while the pips on the outside are fruitlets developed, like the fruitlets of blackberries, from separate carpels. Occasionally the fruit is a composite body, growing from several separate flowers. Pineapples and mulberries are fruits of this type.

Dispersal by wind, water and the plants themselves

None of the fruits or seeds moved by wind, water or a plant's own explosive mechanism need conspicuous colouring. Bright colours would, on the contrary, be a definite drawback for them, since if they attracted animals and were eaten they would almost certainly be destroyed. Nevertheless it is possible for us to appreciate the beauty of their form and construction and sometimes, even, their subtleties of delicate colour.

Wind-dispersed fruits and seeds are small and light or may be assisted by projections which act like wings or parachutes. Of all the tiny wind-dispersed seeds the orchids have the smallest and these float like dust particles in air currents. The orchid's simple system of seed dispersal is quite a contrast to the multitude of intricate mechanisms they use to move their pollen, but even so they manage to be exceptional. The seeds are so small that there are up to a quarter of a million per gramme

and, not surprisingly, species of orchids produce more seeds than any other plant.

The relatively heavy seeds which rely on wind have all sorts of appendages formed from parts of the flower, and designed to catch the wind or help them to float. The ovary wall of the elm expands into a wing with the seed in the middle while in the ash the seed is at one end. Maples have two wings, developed from the wall of a two-carpel ovary. The two sections are fused in the middle so that the fruit is very like an aircraft propeller with the seed at its hub. The Composites often have plumed or parachute-like fruits like the individual stalks that make up the familiar dandelion 'clock'. The seed is enclosed in the little pip at the base of each 'parachute' while the expanded canopy of hairs on the stalk above is formed from a much modified calyx. *Clematis* species have great fluffy balls in which the seeds are transported by the wind. Their tangled appearance has earned them the colloquial names of 'devil's hair' or 'old man's beard'. Pride of place to plants in this category must surely go to cotton. The hairs growing from the surface of the seed die and collapse into twisted spirals as the seeds ripen. The dead tissue is almost pure cellulose and when the individual fibres are twisted and spun, they have a cohesion and elasticity that has been valued by man since 3000 B.C.

Tomato: a true fruit. The flower has a single ovary of five fused carpels each containing several ovules which mature to produce the pips or seeds. The ovary wall grows to form a juicy covering with a waxy outer layer.

Poppy: a true fruit. The flower has an ovary of fused carpels and the ovary wall grows into a dry container. Because the seeds are dispersed by wind it does not need to be brightly coloured.

Raspberry: a true fruit. Each flower has an ovary of several separate carpels, each of which produces a fruitlet. The fruitlets each contain a seed and grow together on the receptacle.

When the flower is mature and fertilization has occurred, a plant directs its energy to producing fruit and seeds. Fruits can be divided into true and false types. True fruits are formed only from the ovary walls, which may expand into a fleshy or hard, dry covering around the seeds. In false fruits another part of the flower, in addition to the ovary, contributes to the structure.

The development of a true fruit
1 Tomato flower ready for fertilization.

2 After fertilization the ovary grows and the petals and stamens fall off as their role has been fulfilled.

3 The ovary wall forms the flesh of the ripe fruit. The seeds inside are dispersed by the animal that eats the fruit.

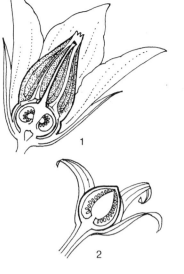

Tumble weeds make the supreme sacrifice to ensure that their seeds are dispersed by the wind. When the seeds are ripe the branches curl so that the whole plant forms a ball, breaks loose from the soil and tumbles over the ground with the wind, shedding seeds as it goes. *Amaranthus graecizans* must be the best known species as it grows in western United States where it has featured in many cowboy adventure films.

Water is used much more to disperse fruits and seeds than it is to distribute pollen. The seeds of plants that grow near water often have a waterproof outer layer encasing air spaces or corky tissue to make them buoyant. The coconut is a water-dispersed fruit, carried on ocean currents. The seed of the coconut is the white edible part and the mature ovary wall develops into the stony protective layer, the buoyant fibres and the waterproof coat. Coconuts are thrown ashore during storms after their sea voyage but they have also been well distributed by man because the plant as a whole is so useful.

Self-dispersal is fairly common in plants. Seeds in pods use this method. As the pod dries it splits open suddenly, forcing out the seeds and sending them some distance from the parent plant. The legumes provide many examples including gorse, broom and the laburnum. The ripe capsules of policeman's helmet plants can be triggered into exploding at the slightest touch. The

Pineapple: a true fruit. The flowers grow clustered together on a spike. After fertilization the ovaries from several separate flowers grow together, their combined walls forming the fruit's flesh.

Strawberry: a false fruit. The flower has several carpels. The fleshy part is the swollen receptacle while the carpels are the small pips on the outside.

Apple: a false fruit. The inner skin around the seeds or pips is formed from the ovary wall. The fleshy outer layer is formed from the swollen receptacle.

Dandelion seeds are dispersed by the wind. The fruit is the little pip or achene at the base of each parachute and once detached from the dandelion 'clock' will float a considerable distance before settling to the ground.

Left: The fruits of the ash have long wings which catch the wind and help disperse the seed to a new site where it will not compete with the parent tree for food and light. The fruits often persist on the tree for many months before they are blown away and can be seen in winter hanging conspicuously among the leafless branches.

The ball of fine hairs surrounding cotton seeds originally evolved to aid their dispersal. Man has used the fibres for so long and selected them for his own purposes that they are now developed beyond the needs of the plant. Without man's sowing techniques they would probably not function efficiently.

Laburnum seeds grow in pods and are dispersed by an explosive mechanism. When ripe, the pods burst open suddenly and twist so that the seeds are flung out. Because no animals are involved, bright colours are not usually a feature of this type of seed dispersal. In fact, laburnum seeds are very poisonous.

Tumbleweed in Chihuahua, northern Mexico. Tumbleweeds have a famous and distinctive method of seed dispersal. When the seeds are ripe the whole plant curls up into a ball, breaks loose from the soil and rolls with the wind. The small fruits drop off the dead plant as it goes.

most famous example of this group of plants must be the squirting cucumber which builds up such tremendous water pressure that when it is triggered it propels the seeds at speeds around 100 km/h over distances of tens of metres. Perhaps this would be better classified as water dispersal!

Dispersal by insects

Most insects are too small to carry fruits or seeds adequately, so they are relatively unimportant as dispersers. Ants are the most frequently used and they can be crucial to the survival of some plants. Since ants' eyesight is poor, the fruits and seeds they move are not usually brightly coloured, although they may attract ants in other ways, by having special outgrowths to provide food, for example. The ants collect the seeds and store them for food but a proportion always remains uneaten and these may germinate successfully.

Dispersal by birds and mammals

There are many vertebrates which help to disperse fruits, ranging from large mammals to reptiles and even fish. However, fruits and seeds that are moved by reptiles and fish are uncommon and we know of no specialized colours used to attract them. Birds are the most important animal dispersal agents, with mammals in second place.

There are two ways in which birds and mammals can act as dispersers. Fruits and seeds may have hooks, sticky hairs or glue which stick to fur or feathers; or they may be edible and so be eaten and carried inside the animal. The dispersal of fruits which stick to the outside of an animal does not usually involve any specially attractive colours but rather depends on accidental encounters as the animal goes about its daily routine.

Different parts of the flower can develop into the structures which stick. Wood avens have hooked styles which remain on the fruit after the rest of the flower has withered away, while cleavers and enchanter's nightshade have hooks developed on the fruit wall. Burdock fruits keep the ring of slender bracts which encircled their composite flower heads. The bracts end in strong, sharp hooks and they are so tenacious that they can be an unpleasant hazard to sheep or long-haired dogs. Each fruit has so many hooks that they can become completely embedded in the animal's coat and cause considerable discomfort. Some fruits have sticky surfaces which stick to birds' bills. *Pisonia brunnoniana* fruits are carried throughout the Pacific region by large birds such as herons and frigatebirds. The fruit's sticky coating is so tenacious that small birds like white-eyes may be unable to get rid of it and so die.

Fruits and seeds which are eaten by animals and dispersed in that way are often brightly coloured. The colour is a signal to the animal that food, in the form of a fleshy seed covering, is present. Some seeds are spat out, but in many cases they pass through the animal's digestive system unharmed. Seeds dispersed like this must be specially adapted to withstand digestive juices. Some, apparently, even benefit from passing through this harsh environment and germinate more freely after being eaten by a bird. One study has shown that 60% of the seeds of broad-leaved pondweed germinated after they had been eaten by ducks, but only 1% developed successfully when they had not been inside a digestive tract.

It is common knowledge that unripe fruits are usually green and not good to eat and it is easy to see why a green colour is used. Green, unripe fruits are hidden amongst the plant's green leaves, away from food-seeking animals. Their bitter or unwholesome taste is a further device used by the plant to prevent the fruit being eaten before the seeds are mature and ready to be dispersed. When fleshy fruits ripen they undergo a series of characteristic changes, such as a rise in sugar content and a general softening. There is usually also a change from green to some contrasting bright colour, the plant's signal that the fruit is ready to eat and the seeds inside are ripe. Occasionally immature fruits may help to attract dispersal animals; the guelder rose, for example, shows a striking contrast between unripe red and ripe black fruits. Though red is an attractive colour to birds, they apparently know in this case that the black fruit is ready to eat and only the ripe fruits are normally taken.

Bird-dispersed fruits are red, orange, yellow, black, white, blue, brown-purple and pink in that order of abundance. This is rather different from the list of colours of flowers that are bird-pollinated, because black fruits are quite common and black is relatively unusual in a bird-pollinated flower. Shininess makes many of these fruit colours even more attractive to birds, and contrast is also important. Red coloured fruits may have some advantage for they will be inconspicuous to many insects which will therefore not be tempted to eat them. Bird-dispersed fruits typically are odourless, as birds lack a sense of smell.

In Chapter 6 we commented on the scarcity of truly red flowers in Europe, where there are no bird pollinators. By contrast, many common European fruits are bright red and as gardeners know to their cost, birds play a very important role in their dispersal. Birds are

The berries of rowan trees are grouped in clusters for greater effect. Their bright colour invites birds to feed on them and so helps to disperse the seeds.

Some plants have unripe fruits of a distinctive colour, providing a contrast with the ripe fruits and making them more attractive. The red unripe and black ripe fruits of this wayfaring tree have attracted a butterfly, but the display is really for the benefit of animals which can disperse the seeds.

Unripe, fleshy fruits are usually green. On ripening the colour changes to one that is attractive to animals, while the taste also often changes from bitter to a more pleasant flavour.

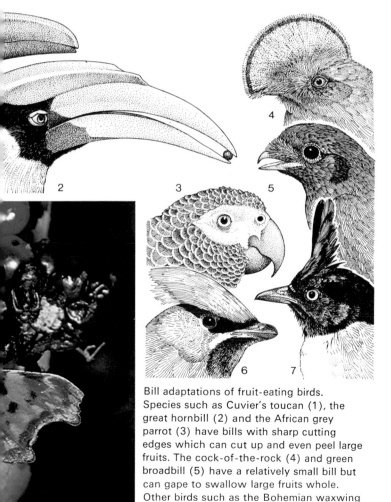

Bill adaptations of fruit-eating birds. Species such as Cuvier's toucan (1), the great hornbill (2) and the African grey parrot (3) have bills with sharp cutting edges which can cut up and even peel large fruits. The cock-of-the-rock (4) and green broadbill (5) have a relatively small bill but can gape to swallow large fruits whole. Other birds such as the Bohemian waxwing (6) and black-crested bulbul (7) have unspecialized bills that are equally suitable for small berries or insects.

especially important as fruit dispersers in the tropics, where there are very few trees using the wind to disperse their fruit. Fruit pigeons, for example, are known to retain seeds as large as nutmegs long enough for them to be transported many kilometres. In the eighteenth century the Dutch attempted to keep a monopoly of the trade in nutmegs and it is said that the reason they failed was that fruit pigeons dispersed the seeds to islands outside the Dutch territories!

Flowerpeckers are a group of birds that feed on both the nectar and fruits of the same plants, so that they are both pollinators and dispersers. They also show within the same family the two methods of feeding that birds use when eating fleshy fruits. One method is to swallow the fruit whole and this is generally used by birds with thin bills. The other system is to chew the flesh away and wipe the seed off the bill onto a branch or twig.

Fruit- and seed-eating birds have evolved appropriate methods of searching for food and special bill shapes. Generally speaking herbivorous birds need a stout, arched bill and they tend to rely on fruit, nuts and seeds rather than foliage. The tough, thick bill of the hawfinch can crush thick-walled fruits, and the short heavily curved bills of some parrots have rasp-like ridges across the inside which can reduce the hardest fruit stones to fragments. The large light beaks of toucans extend the bird's reach without forcing its relatively heavy body into performing acrobatic feats. Their bills also have serrated edges to help them to grasp juicy fruits.

As many as sixty-eight families, and therefore hundreds of species, of fruit-eating birds have been listed as playing some part in seed dispersal, though some are much more effective than others. Most birds are not entirely dependent on fruits for their nutrition and the flesh of most fruits contains only liquid refreshment and carbohydrates. In the tropics, however, some birds live entirely off fruits and nothing else. These birds have co-evolved with the fruits in a very intricate way and accordingly the fruits provide protein, fats and vitamins as well as carbohydrates – in short, all the chemicals necessary for life. Some of the fruits dispersed by these highly specialist birds are green when they are ripe. This disguises them from other birds which would not disperse the seeds efficiently. The behaviour of the special birds that eat them is adapted to searching for green fruits.

Amongst the most specialized mammal fruit-eaters are the bats. In the Old World these include some very large flying mammals such as the flying foxes of Malaya, which may have a wing-span of about one and a half metres. The fruit-eating bats are nocturnal and

The green broadbill's enormous gape is an adaptation to eating large fruits whole. These fruits tend to be scarcer than small berries, but make up for their lack of numbers by their large size and high nutritional value. Because they are so nutritious they are sought out by birds and do not need to advertise themselves with bright colours.

colour blind, so the fruits they visit tend to have pale or dingy colours. The seeds need to be well protected against damage, for bats have sharp teeth. Though their vision is poor, bats have a keen sense of smell and seem to prefer the stale, musty odours bat fruits give off. These smells are not so attractive to humans, but are often worth getting used to since many of the fruits have delicious flesh.

Many other mammals eat and disperse seeds. Some, like the bats, are nocturnal and consequently the fruits they prefer have little in the way of distinctive colours. Where mammals are diurnal, they are attracted to the same colours as birds and may even disperse the same fruits. It therefore seems paradoxical that many colour-

ful fruits should be poisonous to mammals but it is now thought that bird-dispersed fruits sometimes use the same colour signal to advertise both an attractive and an unattractive quality. The plant relies on the animal to make the correct interpretation of its fruit colour either through an innate response or from experience. An example of this is the deadly nightshade, any part of which is poisonous to many mammals. It has been a source of poison from very early times and as little as half a berry has been fatal for a child (though 20-30 berries would be needed to kill a normal adult). But the fruits are eaten with relish by birds and are in fact specifically adapted to dispersal by them. Rabbits, too, can eat the plants without harm but generally speaking the

The masked tanager is typical of many non-specialized birds that exploit the abundant but not very nutritious small berries of trees in the family Melastomaceae. Such birds are very mobile and may carry the seeds of the berries a considerable distance from the parent tree.

Left: Botanically, rosehips are known as false fruits because the red, fleshy parts are swollen receptacles and are not formed from the ovaries. The red hips are attractive to birds and are also a useful source of vitamin C for humans.

Right: Some species of paeony have a colour contrast between fertile and specially evolved sterile seeds. This striking combination makes the seeds very attractive to birds and so helps their dispersal.

The berries of the yew are specialized cones rather than true fruits. The seed is surrounded by a red, fleshy outgrowth or aril to attract the birds which disperse it.

purplish-black colour of the berries is an attractant to birds and a warning colour to mammals.

We use a similar combination of bright advertising and warning colour in medicinal pills. Unfortunately it is not a system which we use efficiently as medicinal pills are dangerous to children and they do not have the necessary experience – nor the innate response – to enable them to interpret the colourful signal correctly. Poisonous fruits use the system more effectively to ensure that only the animals most efficient at dispersing their seeds find their fruits palatable. The advertisement of an unattractive quality by fruits or seeds is one of the few instances of warning colouration in plants, though it is widespread in animals.

The opening fruits of the spindle tree reveal the seeds enclosed in a colourful, fleshy aril which contrasts with the colour of the fruit wall. Most flowering plants with arillate seeds are found in the tropics and the spindle is one of the few which grow in temperate regions.

Left: The akee's large, black seeds contrast both with the fruit wall and with the white, fleshy aril that surrounds them.

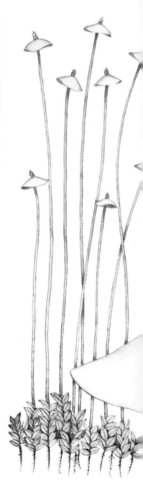

Many mammals which eat fruit do so only as an occasional supplement to their diet. Eland, for instance, eat leaves mainly but take fruits when they are in season. During this time small piles of stones can be found where they have been spat out after the eland has chewed the cud. Monkeys can be very wasteful eaters of fruit and howler monkeys drop as much as half their food without making any attempt to retrieve it. This not only disperses the seeds as the monkeys move through the tree canopies; it also makes them available to ground-feeding mammals which may move them even further or to a more suitable environment.

Plants with coloured seeds

In all the examples discussed so far in this chapter the distinctive colours and other features which attract animals have been in the wall of the fruit. There are, however, some plants where the seeds themselves are the attractive parts and to understand why this is, we must consider some of the evolutionary history of fruit.

It is believed that modern fruit-bearing flowering plants evolved from ancestors with seeds that were not enclosed within ovaries. These ancestral plants belonged to a group called gymnosperms – literally 'naked seed'. There are some modern surviving gymnosperms, including the conifers and cycads, but these are not very closely related to the true ancestors of flowering plants.

These surviving gymnosperms nearly always use wind to move their pollen and seeds but some make use of animals to disperse the seeds. Since they have no outer fruit wall to adapt to attracting animals, they use coloured seeds with pulpy, edible outgrowths called arils. A modern day gymnosperm with arillate seeds is the yew.

The flowering plants, which evolved over 60 million years ago, are called angiosperms, or 'covered seed', a name which refers to the ovary wall surrounding the developing seed. It is often believed that the covering evolved to protect the seeds from the attacks of insects. Because the protective wall masked the colour of the seeds, the fruit itself later took over the attracting role and during the course of evolution the seeds tended to lose their colour. However, some flowering plants are less evolutionarily advanced and many of these still have their brightly coloured seeds, often with an aril that is eaten by animals. There are also intermediate stages where an ovary wall has developed, but the aril remains covering the seed. In these plants the fruit wall opens when it is ripe to reveal the seeds, and may have no function in dispersal, though it does perhaps provide a contrasting colour to the colour of the seeds. Several fully developed fruits have colourful seeds without arils. One of the paeonies, *Paeonia obovata* is especially striking since there is a most unusual colour effect be-

The fruiting body of a phalloid fungus in the rainforests of central America has a delicate net which may make the fungus more attractive to flies. The flies lick the mass of spores at the tip of the fungus and carry spores away on their feet.

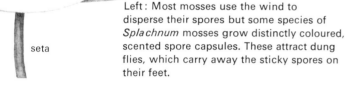

spores

capsule

seta

Left: Most mosses use the wind to disperse their spores but some species of *Splachnum* mosses grow distinctly coloured, scented spore capsules. These attract dung flies, which carry away the sticky spores on their feet.

tween red sterile seeds and blue fertile ones. The sterile seeds cannot develop into new plants and apparently develop simply for contrast with the normal fertile ones.

The genus *Sterculia* includes several plants with primitive fruits containing coloured arillate seeds. In these, the ovary wall develops into a star of five fleshy arms which opens to reveal the ripe seeds. The seeds are covered at least partially with pulpy aril, coloured red, orange or yellow which is particularly attractive to birds. Perhaps the most widely known plant with arillate seeds is the nutmeg. Its fruits are like small peaches with an orange coloured fruit wall surrounding a seed with a brilliant red fibrous aril. The red aril tissue, when dried, is the spice mace and the seed it contains is the commercial nutmeg. Most arillate-seeded plants are tropical, but some belonging to the genus *Euonymus* grow in temperate regions. The spindle tree, whose wood was used to make spindles for the textile industry, is native to Europe and Asia. It has red or pink fruit walls with white seeds and orange arils. The burning-bush plant of the same genus from North America has a scarlet fruit with brown seeds inside scarlet arils.

A famous fruit with arillate seeds is the durian. The fruit is spherical, up to about 20cms in diameter, and is heavily armoured with sharp-pointed spikes. The fruit tissue smells unpleasant to most humans and encases brown seeds, each with a cream-coloured custard-like

aril. It appeals to a wide range of mammals, which locate the fruit by its very distinctive smell. It is apparently eaten by gibbons, monkeys, bears, squirrels, and orang-utans while it hangs in the tree and by tigers, pigs, deer, tapir, rhinoceros, ants and beetles when it drops to the ground. But man must be its greatest admirer. The naturalist Alfred Russell Wallace maintained in 1869 that 'to eat durians is a new sensation, worth a voyage to the East to experience'!

Spore-dispersal in fungi and mosses

The use of animals for dispersal is not quite restricted to seed plants. Ferns, fungi, moss and lichens produce spores, not seeds, and usually use wind, water or self-dispersal. There are, however, a few fascinating examples of colours being used to attract animals for spore dispersal.

One group of fungi, the phalloids, have become specialized for attracting flies to move their spores. The stinkhorn has its spores on the tip of its stalk, clustered in a black mass which is attractive to flies. The attraction is increased by a powerful and, to us, unpleasant smell. In fact it uses very similar methods to the flowers which mimic bad meat to attract fly pollinators (see Chapter 5). The flies lick off all the spores in a matter of hours, so the fungi are frequently seen without their black tip. Some of the stinkhorn's tropical relatives have a stalk enclosed in a beautiful network crinoline which probably helps to attract flies. Other tropical phalloids have sterile scarlet rays radiating from the top of the stalk. These may function in the same way as petals in flowers, focusing attention on the central spore mass.

Outside the phalloids, insect dispersal of fungal spores is relatively rare although it occurs in many unrelated groups and has presumably evolved independently in each. Other fungi use scent to attract their animal visitors, not colour. Some rust fungi, e.g. *Puccinia graminis*, cause their host to exude a distinctive, sweetish smell and a drop of sugary liquid which gathers the spores within it as it forms. Insects are attracted to the sweet liquid and after eating it carry off the spores to colonize another area. The famous underground truffles also use scent, but their smell attracts mammals which can dig down to them. Their spores are released as the fruiting body is eaten. This kind of use of scent means that no special colouring is needed.

There is a single known case of insects being used to disperse moss spores. Some species belonging to the genus *Splachnum* have red or yellow coloured scented capsules which attract dung flies to disperse their sticky spores.

Plants that use colour for camouflage and disguise

Camouflage and mimicry are widely developed to a fascinating and almost unbelievably accurate degree in animals and are used for many different purposes. In plants they are much less common and much less well known but, as we shall see, play a useful part in the plant's survival.

Camouflage

An organism is said to be camouflaged when it blends into its background. For most plants camouflage is impossible, since their leaves must be well exposed in order to capture sunlight. Instead of attempting to disguise their leaves, plants have evolved other defence mechanisms against herbivores such as being foul-tasting or poisonous, covering themselves with spines and prickles or stinging hairs, or even employing fierce ants to guard them. Nevertheless there are instances where plants can be described as using camouflage techniques.

We saw in the last chapter how unripe fruits and those not dispersed by animals hang inconspicuously among the leaves of the plant. Animal-pollinated flowers are also often green when they are immature, and this may be another example of camouflage.

Some plants live in environments where green, leafy camouflage would be absurd. There is a group of plants in desert areas of south and south-west Africa which manage to blend into their surroundings to a remarkable degree and are only obvious when they are in flower. *Pleiospilos bolusii* has pitted, coarse leaves very like fragments of stones and the leaves of *Titanopsis calcarea* are a crusty white like their limestone environment. The chief group of these plants is the fifty or so species of stone plants of the genus *Lithops*. Stone plants are small with two leaves more or less fused together. They are

Insectivorous plants such as these Venus flytraps and sundews are typical of areas where the soil is very poor in nitrogen. They obtain an ample supply of amino acids by attracting and killing insects. Venus flytraps mimic the red colour of flowers to lure their prey while sundews have leaf hairs with small, glistening knobs which attract flies. When the insect alights on the special leaves, it sticks fast and is digested by juices secreted by the hairs.

very resistant to drought as they carry an ample supply of water in their swollen leaves and can survive without rain for many months. Unfortunately there seems to be a shortage of detailed field observations on stone plants and it is still not known if they gain any real protection by looking so much like pebbles. When we see them displayed in botanic gardens their camouflage is certainly effective but this may be at least partly due to the fact that their surroundings are specially chosen to fit them rather than the other way around. However, in a desert environment a succulent food plant must be eagerly sought after and in a situation where food supplies are very limited a good protective camouflage could be of considerable advantage.

Another way of being camouflaged is to become small and lost among the surrounding vegetation and this seems to be the system adopted by the sensitive plants of the *Mimosa* genus. *Mimosa pudica* is a popular household novelty because when touched, it collapses and folds its leaves. In tropical America we have seen mimosas collapsing in open fields when disturbed by the hooves and lips of grazing cattle. Because the leaf area is reduced the plant becomes very inconspicuous, particularly to cattle, whose eyesight is mediocre. If left undisturbed, the plant raises its leaves and the leaflets spread out again; the temporary ducking for cover seems a useful compromise between needing the sun and needing to survive. Its behaviour is, however, not well understood – it also closes at night and during cold weather and it can even be anaesthetized by ether or chloroform so that it will not respond to touch.

Batesian mimicry in plants

When one organism gains a one-sided advantage by imitating another organism more numerous than itself, it is said to be a Batesian mimic. In animals this is quite common but there are also a number of cases of plant mimicry which can be considered in the same way.

One important reason plants use mimicry is as a protection against animals that eat them. A recent study by Larry E. Gilbert has revealed what appear to be subtle examples of one plant imitating another, to its advantage. The larvae of Heliconid butterflies feed on passion flower leaves. Gilbert points out that the leaves of some passion flowers resemble in shape and shade of green the leaves of unrelated plants which are known to be either distasteful or even poisonous to the larvae. Presumably at least a proportion of female butterflies will mistake the passion flower leaves for poisonous leaves and will not lay their eggs on them. A number of other examples of similar leaf shapes and colours have been

reported and it may be a phenomenon of more widespread significance than is usually realized.

Gilbert has also observed an even more remarkable example of mimicry: some passion flower leaves have mimic butterfly eggs on their surface. The caterpillars of Heliconid butterflies eat the leaves on which they are born but they are also cannabalistic and eat any newly-hatched larvae that they find. The female butterfly must therefore make sure that the eggs are laid where this will not happen, so if she finds a leaf which appears to be already occupied, she will move elsewhere. The chances of the leaf being eaten are thus reduced, in spite of its palatability.

Man has inadvertently selected some weed mimics of crops in his cultivation of food plants. Man acts like a predator on weeds and it is to the weeds' advantage if they can resemble the crop. Some weeds have developed seeds which behave similarly to the crop in the seed-cleaning processes used by man to select good seeds. For example winnowing machines are used to fan flax seeds and husks and blow them different distances so that they can be separated. Seeds of gold of pleasure, a common weed of flax, have evolved a size and weight which makes them fall in the same place as flax seeds. In fact their size and weight are different from flax seeds, but it is the combination that is important in winnowing and in this case weed and crop seeds both have similar

Left: Like many young fruits, immature baobab fruits are green and hang well camouflaged among the green foliage of the tree. Animals looking for food will therefore not see them until they are ripe and ready for dispersal.

Below: Pebble plants in a botanic garden look amazingly like the small stones among which they grow. In the wild, their camouflage may not be so perfect but it probably helps to conceal them from grazing animals.

The dark rim and bad smell of the pitcher plant mimic rotting meat to attract flies to their slippery inner walls. Like other insectivorous plants, they use insects to supplement their supply of nutrients from the poor soil in which they grow.

aerodynamic properties. The weed is therefore sown with the crop and survives another year.

Some weeds, it is thought, have become such efficient mimics of crop plants that they have become crops in their own right! It is believed that rye and oats may have arisen in this way in early wheat fields. In poor climates or soils, the hardier 'weed' crops would be greatly favoured and hence further developed once their food value had been recognized by the farmers.

Mimicry in insectivorous plants

A number of plants that live in habitats where the soil lacks nutrients – such as bogs – supplement their supplies of essential chemicals by capturing insects and slowly digesting them. Wolfgang Wickler believes that in some cases they use mimicry to lure the insects to them.

Some pitcher plants coax insects into a reservoir in which they drown and rot. In some species, around the entrance to the pitcher there are markings reminiscent of rotting meat and these, together with a bad smell, probably attract the flies. The famous venus fly-trap has trap-like leaves which close on small flies that land on them. The leaves are red on their inner surface and when they are open, their colour, together with the open jaws of the trap, may look sufficiently like a flower to deceive small insects.

The Venus flytrap is a native of the south-eastern United States, but is now widely grown as a houseplant. Insects such as this unfortunate bee are lured by colour and smell to explore a trap formed from modified leaves. When small trigger hairs are touched in the right way the trap closes and digestive juices begin to soften the prey. When all the nutrients have been extracted, the trap reopens, ready to operate again.

It is interesting to notice that a successful 'pollination mimic' must deceive an animal twice to achieve a transfer of pollen: once to brush the pollen on, and a second time to receive it. In other cases of Batesian mimicry, involving animal predators and prey, a single successful deception is to the mimic's advantage.

Mimicry in seed dispersal

We saw in the last chapter how certain fungi and mosses attract flies to disperse their spores. It is not clear if the flies receive any reward and if they do not, they may be examples of Batesian mimicry. Some flowering plants certainly have seeds which deceive birds and mammals into thinking they are providing food because they look like commonly eaten fruits. The best known examples are found among some tropical legumes. These have fairly large, hard, shiny seeds, usually bright scarlet or red, or bi-coloured red and black – all colours associated with bird dispersal. Though they look good to eat they have no fleshy, nutritious part and the plants do not have to divert their resources to provide it. In some cases the mimicry is accompanied by extra visual attractions. The seeds of *Adenanthera pavonina* are made even more conspicuous because they are in yellow pods and some *Rhynchosia* species have red petals which persist until the seeds are ripe, so adding more colour.

The geographical distribution of the mimics and the fruit models seems to prove that this is a true example of mimicry. The wholly red seeds and the wholly red nutritious fruits grow in the same areas while the bi-coloured red and black seeds are found with the red and black fruits they resemble. If mimicry does occur and the seeds and fruit are successfully dispersed by the same agent, then the two plants should naturally have the same distribution. The fact that this does happen with two different sets of mimics and their models can hardly be coincidence.

Although this subject has only recently been studied more than superficially, it seems that hard fruit and seed mimics occur in several families, in temperate as well as tropical areas. It is a type of mimicry that provides an interesting contrast with mimicry in the animal world. There, animals use mimicry to avoid being eaten; plants, on the other hand, use it to make sure they are swallowed, if not digested!

Müllerian mimicry

Müllerian mimicry occurs when a number of species which look alike, and are equally numerous, have evolved a common advertising style which works to their mutual advantage.

These red and black mimetic seeds hint to birds that they are fleshy and succulent. The birds are tricked into swallowing the seeds and so disperse them. In fact seeds of this type are usually quite indigestible and often so hard that they are used to make beads.

There are a number of cases where several different species with similar flower shapes and colours grow together in one region. Because they look similar, they all attract similar pollinators and so increase each others' chances of being successfully fertilized. A common advertising style should work best where the flowers are unspecialized so that many animals can take advantage of all the available flowers. Possible examples occur in the Alps, where alpine buttercups, mountain avens, and the alpine moon-daisy all have flowers of similar size and shape, all largely white in colour and all pollinated by unspecialized insects.

According to one theory plant colours may be characteristic of certain areas and this may give them all some advantage. The arctic and sub-arctic have a high proportion of white flowers, deserts a high proportion of yellows, mountains and humid places blues. Sometimes there is a seasonal preponderance of a particular colour, which may be connected with the colour preferences of the insects that are around at that time of year. In the Baltic region studies have shown that white flowers predominate in April and May, but are rare in autumn. May is the month when yellow flowers are at their commonest and there is a second peak of yellows in October. Reddish colours are found most often in September while violets and blues occur in more or less the same proportions all through the flowering seasons with a slight peak in the autumn.

One of the most perfect examples of Müllerian mimicry in plants occurs in North America, where the majority of hummingbird-pollinated flowers are red. Further south in tropical America there is more variety in their colours. K. A. Grant has suggested an intriguing explanation. He believes that the red North American flowers are pollinated by hummingbirds which are migrating and thus constantly moving to new areas and different flowers. It helps the hummingbird to recognize the sources of nectar in strange places if all the flowers are similarly coloured – and it therefore helps the flowers to be fertilized if they are all the same colour. In the tropical areas, hummingbirds are resident and have time to learn about the individual species which therefore can develop a wide range of colours.

Müllerian mimicry may also be involved in the large numbers of similarly coloured fruits which are produced by plants of temperate regions in autumn. Usually red or black, their common advertising colour makes them more conspicuous and attractive than they would be if each species looked different. Many are also eaten by birds migrating south from the arctic and they, like the hummingbirds of North America, will easily recognize similarly coloured food sources as they journey.

The *Lantana* (left) and *Asclepias* species (above) from central America are Müllerian mimics: they use the same orange and yellow combination of colours to attract similar pollinators and increase each other's chances of being fertilized. The *Epidendrum* orchid (right) is a Batesian mimic of the other two flowers. It uses the same colour signal to attract the Heliconid butterfly pollinator but produces no nectar or pollen on which it can feed.

Man's influence on plant colours

Man (or his close relatives) has been on Earth for hundreds of thousands of years and, like all other animals, has always been dependent on green plants for his existence. Primitive man led a life of hunting and gathering and ate animals (usually herbivores) and any edible plant parts he could find. Such a way of life was not only hazardous but meant that much of the time he was awake was spent searching for food. Hunting and gathering populations were invariably very small and their impact on plants in general and the colours of plants in particular was only slight.

One of the great turning points of human history occurred in an area called the Fertile Crescent (an area of land stretching from the Eastern Mediterranean, around the headwaters of the Euphrates and Tigris, through to the Persian Gulf) about 8000 B.C. Here for the first time man consciously began to domesticate wild plants for crops and began the so-called agricultural revolution. Rice and wheat in the Old World and maize in the New, were developed into the staple foods of today. Man the cultivator was assured of a supply of food and was able to lead a much more stable existence than the hunters and gatherers. The development of towns and cities and the rise of the great civilizations followed the development of crop cultivation. Man still depended on green plants for his food, of course, but they were now utilized much more efficiently. Man's population increased gradually and with it his cultivation of more diverse crops and eventually of ornamental plants. The impact of man on plants has continued at an increasing pace and in many different ways.

The colours of crop plants

Crops are grown for their economic value rather than from any desire to produce colourful effects. Nevertheless striking colours can be associated with them.

The warm gold of ripe wheat has been a welcome sight at the close of summer for hundreds of years. The rich expanse of the crop is a result of a great deal of selective breeding from the low yielding grasses that were the ancestors of modern grains. It is perhaps disappointing to realize that the colouring is the result of dead plant tissue !

Colours occur, for no obvious reason, in vegetables such as beetroot, carrots, radishes and red cabbage. Many of the fruits grown in the temperate parts of the world are brightly coloured, a relic of the days when they were wild and had to be dispersed by birds. Where crops are cultivated on a large scale the colour effects can be quite beautiful. A golden field of ripe corn has been the subject of many paintings but probably few of the artists paused to consider they were simply observing a mass of mainly dead plant tissue from which chlorophyll had disappeared and which was pigmented with oxidized chemicals. Our own favourite cultivated landscape is the deep green of neat tea estates on tropical hillsides.

A fast disappearing feature of cereal fields is the beautiful array of weed species associated with them. A field of poppies is a fine sight and their splendid reds among the corn have been regarded in the past as the life blood sprouting from the soil. The perfect complement to poppies are the blues of cornflowers and yellows of charlocks. Their bright colours stand out from the growing corn as vivid signals to pollinators. But modern methods of seed cleaning and herbicidal control, perhaps combined with increasingly competitive strains of crop, have reduced these weeds in some countries to the status of rarities.

The symptoms of nutrient deficiencies

A less attractive type of colour seen amongst crop plants is caused when they are short of nutrients. Man has cultivated plants so that they grow in an unnatural way. They are grown to produce a maximum yield and so need more mineral nutrients than wild plants. When one of these nutrients is in short supply the plants show signs of distress – they literally go 'off colour'. The type of colour developed can be useful to the grower as it helps him to diagnose the cause and shows which chemical treatment is needed to correct it.

The leaves of most plants turn yellowish-green if they are short of nitrogen, but other mineral deficiencies can have different effects on different plant species. Tobacco leaves show magnesium deficiency by turning light yellow, while cotton turns dark red-purple. When Alsike clover is short of iron the tips of its leaves turn purplish but *Eucalyptus* leaves go golden brown. Sometimes the colour change is localized and makes the leaves look mottled. When alfalfa is starved of potassium, for example, it develops yellow and red-brown leaf mottles.

In general 'off colour' plants suffering from nutrient deficiencies are much less common in the wild. Presumably wild plants are well adapted to the places in which they grow and do not so easily lose their natural greenness. Nevertheless some instances are well known. On some lime-rich soils plants may undergo a seasonal yellowing in spring, probably caused by an iron deficiency. Iron is necessary for the proper production of chlorophyll, so if there is not enough iron the plant will not make enough green pigment.

The chemical content in the soil is not the only thing that influences plant colours: too much or too little water, low or high temperatures and disease all bring about colour changes.

Plant dyes

Plants which produce dyes have long been cultivated for their colours, or rather for the coloured substances that can be obtained from them. Plant dyes have now largely been superseded by synthetic chemicals but they are still used on a small scale and there are always connoisseurs who claim that the older dyes give superior colours. It takes much longer to dye with plant colours but they give a soft, lustrous colouring and are very long lasting. Even when very old, plant colours retain their beauty: old tapestries fade gradually in a uniform way, not in

Eucalyptus was planted experimentally to cover old mine wastes in Rhodesia, but was found to need expensive boron supplements if it was to grow successfully. The brown mottling on these *Eucalyptus* leaves is a symptom of boron deficiency.

Corn poppies in a field treated with herbicides show several colour variations. Normal red poppies appear ultra-violet to pollinating bees, which cannot see red; their stamens and the dark markings at the petals' base appear black.

patches like fabrics dyed with manufactured dyes.

Of the very large number of plant dyes three are particularly famous. Indigo, a beautiful blue dye, is produced from the indigo plant. Its leaves contain a colourless substance which is converted to blue dye when the foliage is crushed in water. Turkey red, a magnificent red dye, comes from the roots of a madder and still finds a small market for use in artists' paints. Finally, the plant dye litmus is still widely used in schools. Generations of children have been introduced to chemistry by adding vinegar (a weak acid) to paper dyed with litmus and watching the change from blue to red.

Ornamental plants

Ornamental plants originated about 4-5000 years ago, when man, made prosperous by his food crops, began to cultivate plants purely for decoration. The art was most advanced and most varied first in India and China, partly because of the artistic sensibility of the eastern people, partly because the warm climate provided a constant supply of brilliantly coloured wild flowers.

Religion has often encouraged the development of ornamental plants. Buddhism, for example, required people to offer flowers rather than sacrifice animals and so organized a cult of flowers which is still most highly developed in places where Buddhism has flourished. On the other hand Mohammedan power barred the way between Europe and the flower cultures of the East throughout the Middle Ages. It was only in the sixteenth century that decorative plants began to be moved westwards to Italy, Holland, England and France. There, university gardens opened in swift succession to receive the new plants, gradually changing into the botanic gardens of today. During the reign of George III, under the guidance of Sir Joseph Banks, 7000 new plant species were brought to England, most of them ornamental. They included two extremely important species, *Rosa chinensis* and *Chrysanthemum indicum*, which have contributed enormously to the development of the modern rose and chrysanthemum.

This movement of specimens across the world has been one of man's major influences on plants. It has continued right up to the present time and is still going on today. The large numbers of plants arriving in experimental centres have also provided raw material for artificial selection and have led to the two other major ways in which man has influenced economic and decorative plants – his continuous selection of plants with improved qualities and his deliberate or accidental interbreeding or hybridization between varieties, species or even genera.

Man selected and hybridized by hit and miss methods long before he understood quite what he was doing. Plant selection and breeding had been going on for hundreds of years before the science of heredity or genetics as it is called was founded. The first person to carry out conclusive experiments which explained the logic of plant breeding was the monk Gregor Johann Mendel who worked in the mid-nineteenth century in a monastery garden in Brno, in what is now Czechoslovakia. Like many monks in those days he was a specialist in several fields. He was a student of botany and mathematics and both subjects helped him tremendously in producing the theories on heredity, published in 1860.

Mendel worked on the inheritance of a range of features or characters in the cultivated pea. Amongst his experiments was a study of red and white flowered peas, both of which were common. The pea flower turned out to be the perfect choice for an experimental study. Its flower is fairly large and is constructed so that it is relatively easy to pollinate by hand. The anthers of each flower are quite easy to remove so that self-pollination can be prevented. In one of his experiments Mendel crossed large numbers of red flowered peas with large numbers of white flowered ones.

All the seedlings that grew from this red × white cross had red flowers. The red was said to be dominant to white and the plants were called F_1 hybrids. These first generation (F_1) plants were then crossed amongst themselves and the plants of the second (F_2) generation were 75% red and 25% white. Mendel called the characters (here the white colour) that had disappeared in the F_1 plants and reappeared in the F_2 plants 'recessive characters'.

Mendel explained that each plant flower colour was determined by a factor (we now call it a gene) which existed in two forms (now called alleles). In the red flowers used at the beginning of the experiment these two alleles were labelled WW and in the white flowers ww. When the plants were crossed the new F_1 plants contained one allele from each parent – Ww. The allele for red colour (W) is dominant over that for white colour (w) so red, not white flowers appeared. When these plants were crossed among themselves, the alleles were sorted randomly and the second generation F_2 plants included WW, Ww and ww types. The 25% with two white alleles (the wws) were white; the other 75% (the

Mutant white bluebells occur occasionally in most bluebell populations when a plant fails to produce anthocyanin pigments. It is not known how this affects their chances of pollination.

Right: Polyanthus as a whole arise from a cross between the primrose *Primula vulgaris* and the cowslip *P. veris*. A blue primrose was introduced from the Himalayas and the new colour strains are mutants that have been produced from the original hybrid. The flowers here belong to the Pacific Coast strain, developed along America's western coast. They are less hardy than European polyanthus and breeders are now trying to introduce European hardiness into the American strain.

WWs and the Wws) were all red. Like the Wws of the first generation cross, the new Ww plants contained both a red and a white allele but were coloured red because red is dominant to white.

Mendel's studies, the work of a great genius, were published in a rather obscure journal and it was forty years before they began to be developed by the geneticists of our own century.

We now know that inheritance of plant colours, and inheritance in general, is not always as simple as it was in Mendel's peas. For example dominant and recessive characters are not always so clear cut. In the snapdragon, a cross between red and white produces pink flowers in the F_1 generation – a mixture of the colours of its two parents. When the pink flowers are crossed, the F_2 plants have 25% red flowers, 25% white flowers and 50% pink flowers, showing that although the colours may blend in the plants, the genes themselves retain their identity. Another complication occurs when genes have more than two alleles, for each may have a different effect on colour.

Sometimes characters are not determined by a single gene and its alleles but by a number of genes acting together. When this happens the characters tend to vary continuously instead of being sharply distinct as they are in the red and white peas. In wheat grains, for example, there is a whole range of colours from dark red to white, controlled by four genes in different combinations.

Some features of inheritance are more difficult to explain and are often very complex. Nevertheless Mendel's simple experiments showed several basic principles and selection and hybridization to produce plant colours are still founded on these.

Sometimes changes take place in the genes themselves as they produce their alleles and these changes are known as mutations. Mutations are usually harmful to the plant but sometimes a mutant plant may appeal to horticulturists and plant breeders can take advantage of it. Often a new character turns up in an otherwise unattractive plant and the breeder will then try to combine it with more desirable characters from other plants.

Mutations occur naturally at widely different frequencies for some genes mutate much more rapidly than others. If mutants do not appear rapidly, modern breeders sometimes resort to rather sinister techniques to obtain the changes. In chrysanthemums, for example, pink flowered plants have been subjected to gamma radiation from a radioactive source, producing bronze mutants in the next generation. When the bronze plants were irradiated and crossed, they produced a yellow flowered variety. The radiation may mutate any of the

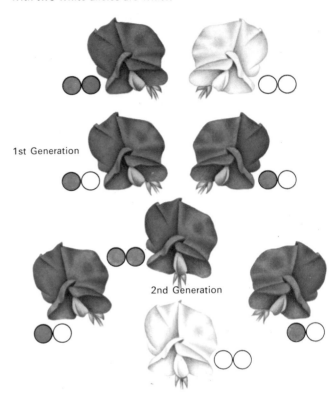

When a red-flowered pea is crossed with a white one, their offspring have only red flowers. Each first generation plant has both red and white alleles, but red is dominant. When these plants are crossed among themselves, they produce three red flowers to every white one. Because red is still dominant, only the plants with two white alleles are white.

1st Generation

2nd Generation

genes, not just those carrying colour, and may kill or damage the plant. Usually, however, some of the mutants are attractive and the breeder selects these, discarding the rest of the commercially unsuitable survivors.

A very large number of ornamental plants have been produced over the last four hundred years. Some have involved selection and breeding within a single species, others selection and breeding between several species. The examples given below illustrate the complicated ways in which the colours we see in our gardens arose and have been developed by horticulturalists.

The hyacinths grown in such numbers in homes, gardens and nurseries every winter have all been derived from one species, the tall, elegant *Hyacinthus orientalis*, which was introduced to Holland from the Lebanon or Taurus mountains about 1560. The wild species, with its loose spikes of blue flowers, still exists in its native habitat. In the first century of cultivation white, pink and double forms appeared and were selected, then deep crimson, lilac and yellow. The shape of the spike was changed by breeding from plants that showed natural mutations, and the numbers of flowers and leaves increased. By 1768 there were nearly 2000 named varieties. Because fashion has changed over the years, most of these have been lost and now not many more than a hundred varieties survive.

The sweet pea's history is in many ways similar to that of the hyacinths. Seeds of the first sweet pea were sent to Enfield near London from their native Sicily in 1699. These original plants had reddish-purple flowers. Up to 1886 only four mutations had appeared, and all of these were recessive, disappearing temporarily when the plants were crossed. The four mutants had white, pink, dark maroon and brilliant red flowers. In the next twenty-five years or so a whole group of changes arose and from these were bred the range of colours in the tall, large-flowered, somewhat less scented sweet peas of modern horticulture. It is still not known why there was suddenly a flush of new mutants near the turn of the century after nearly two hundred years of stability in the species.

In some plants the production of the range of modern flowers has involved selective breeding and hybridization on a large, complicated scale. The history of modern rhododendrons and cultivated orchids is particularly complex, for example. One of today's most popular garden flowers, the rose, has also been selectively bred.

Roses have a very long history of cultivation although the history of modern garden roses does not really begin until the start of the nineteenth century. At this time independently cultivated roses from the Far East were imported into the West and began to be hybridized with those of Europe and western Asia. One example will show the time and care needed to breed a new colour into a rose, in this case to produce a yellow hybrid tea.

Monsieur Pernet-Ducher from Lyons in France had tried for many years to breed a true yellow into the hybrid tea type of rose, which had white, pink and red varieties but no good yellow. He began to succeed in 1888 when he managed to obtain fertile seed from a cross between the Persian yellow rose *Rosa foetida* and a red hybrid perpetual rose 'Antoine Ducher'. One seedling grew into a plant with flowers the shape of 'Antoine Ducher' and petals which were orange-red on the inside and yellow outside like the Persian yellow rose. This plant was then crossed with a number of hybrid tea roses and the first product to be marketed, 'Soleil d'Or', had orange petals splashed with red. This was the first of a new generation of roses. In 1910 it was crossed with a hybrid tea rose 'Mme Melanie Soupert' to produce the first pure yellow hybrid tea type rose, 'Rayon d'Or'. Many more hybridizations were carried out and this was the beginning of many of the brilliant colourings in present-day garden roses. The yellow, orange and flame colours in modern rose gardens are largely derived from 'Soleil d'Or', the original hybrid produced by Pernet-Ducher.

Rose breeders have been trying for many years to produce a range of blue roses. This is difficult because the rose has no blue flowered relatives which can be crossed with the cultivated group. However, the close chemical similarities between red and blue anthocyanin pigments make the production of a blue rose theoretically possible. By constantly selecting mutant flowers with a suggestion of blue, and crossing them with one another, rose breeders have gone a long way towards achieving it. There are some very respectable violets and lavenders and we may expect good blues to be developed over the next few decades. As each cross takes at least a year to bloom, the process is one that cannot be greatly hurried. Whether blue roses will ever prove to be really popular other than as novelties is another question.

There is a very curious story in the history of tulip breeding. In old books and flower paintings, tulips are often shown with irregular, sharply defined splashes of contrasting colours, called broken colours. Contemporary written descriptions explain that the particular variety was bred then 'broken' by its breeder a few years later. What happened was that when two tulips with markings were crossed, the offspring were all dull and dark. After a few years, the colours would suddenly 'break' and produce beautifully marked flowers. People tried all kinds of ways to get their tulips to break immediately but none was successful.

The explanation is that the markings were due to infection by a virus, which does little harm to the health of the plant. The virus is not carried in the seed, so the offspring of broken tulip crosses were plain coloured at first. Sooner or later a greenfly would carry the virus from a 'broken' tulip to a healthy one, and the markings would then appear. Once the plant was infected, the markings would appear on the flower every year. Each tulip variety reacted to the virus in a different way and for a time broken tulips were very fashionable. Their popularity then diminished, though in recent years there has been a revival of interest in them. One widely grown group of broken tulips are the 'Rembrandts' with varieties such as the brown and yellow 'Absalon', purple and cream 'May bloom' and salmon-pink and cream 'Zomerschoon'.

As plant breeders try to improve flower colours they also often select plants with unusually large flowers or with 'double flowers'. There are two types of double flowers. Sometimes the stamens and/or the carpels of the flower may fail to develop properly and may instead take the shape and colour of the petals. When the conversion is only partial the flowers are called semi-double. Breeders who try to use these doubling genes run into problems because fully double flowers, having neither pollen-producing stamens nor egg-containing carpels, are completely sterile. In practice, however, the flower will usually have some unaltered stamens or carpels

Tulips have been a popular flower with both breeders and gardeners for a very long time. These painted lady tulips, widely cultivated in Europe, also grow wild in the Himalayas.

Coleus is one of the most spectacular of all variegated houseplants. The patterns on the leaf surface are areas of different anthocyanin development and defective chlorophyll. This type of variegation can be inherited.

Man has not only influenced the size, colour and taste of apples, he has also modified the tree shape to make it more accessible. Individual trees are small but the yield for a particular area of orchard is greater than when it contained old-fashioned trees.

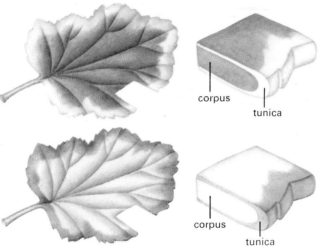

corpus

tunica

corpus

tunica

In leaves made up of two layers of cells, green and white variegation may be caused by defective chloroplasts. In a green leaf with white edges, the inner layer of cells, the corpus, is normal (green) but the outer layer, the tunica, lacks chloroplasts. At the centre, the inner green layer shows through the outer layer of cells. At the edge of the leaf there is only one layer of cells, the defective outer layer, so here the leaf looks white. In a white leaf with green edges, it is the inner layer of cells that is defective.

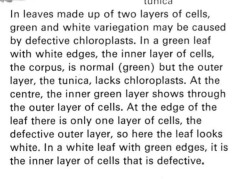

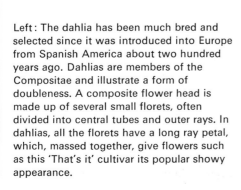

Left: The dahlia has been much bred and selected since it was introduced into Europe from Spanish America about two hundred years ago. Dahlias are members of the Compositae and illustrate a form of doubleness. A composite flower head is made up of several small florets, often divided into central tubes and outer rays. In dahlias, all the florets have a long ray petal, which, massed together, give flowers such as this 'That's it' cultivar its popular showy appearance.

and the breeder can often get doubles to produce seeds either as the male or female parent. In some cases completely sterile doubles have remained in cultivation for hundreds of years by planting cuttings or dividing. The double daffodil 'Van Sion', which has been cultivated since the eighteenth century is one of these. Often, however, stocks propagated in this way are lost through virus infections.

A quite separate form of doubleness occurs in the Compositae, in plants such as dahlias, chrysanthemums and zinnias. As we saw in Chapter 4, composite flower heads may have both tube (central) and ray (outer) florets, both of which may be fully fertile. Double versions of these flowers have heads of outer, ray florets only. They occur naturally in the dandelion and have been produced by selective breeding in cultivated composite flowers.

Man's influence on ornamental plant colours has not been confined to flowers. He has also cultivated plants with beautifully coloured fruits and with decorative foliage – the so-called variegated plants In variegated leaves, some of the green chlorophyll pigmented area is masked, and so the area available for photosynthesis is reduced. Plants with variegated leaves would probably therefore be at a disadvantage in nature, but man has often deliberately selected and propagated them.

Variegations in leaves can be caused in a large number of ways. In plants like some begonias, spotted dog plants and the aluminium plant, the silvery spots and streaks are simply air blisters under the outer layer of cells. Sometimes the chloroplasts, which contain chlorophyll, are defective in parts or the whole of leaves. The beautiful *Coleus blumei* from Java, has additional anthocyanin patterns as well as defective chloroplasts. Numerous varieties of this species have been cultivated with leaf patterns of red, bronze, brown, purple, yellow, white and shades of green. In spotted laurel and varieties of

107

Codiaeum variegatum, the defective chloroplasts are in small, localized areas and give a spotting effect.

These two types of leaf variegation can be inherited through the seed but in a number of cases the patterns are the result of defects which cannot be inherited in the usual way. In these cases the variegation can only be maintained from cuttings. In many plants the stem, leaf and flower cells are arranged in two layers, a thin outer layer (the tunica) and an inner layer (the corpus). The two layers remain separate as they mature and it is possible for one layer to have defective chloroplasts, while the other is normal. This is the case with, for example, variegated pelargoniums which can have either white edges to green leaves or green edges to white leaves.

In a green leaf with white edges, the inner layer of cells is green, but is enveloped by a defective, white-celled tunica. Over most of the leaf the tunica is only one cell thick, so the green shows through, hiding the white colour. At the edges, however, the tunica is thicker and without an inner layer of green corpus cells, so forms a white border. A white leaf with green edges has the same basic structure, but here the underlying corpus is defective. Its white colour shows through the green except at the edges of the leaf.

Sometimes a section of both tunica and corpus are faulty, causing sections of variegation. In plants with parallel veins such as grasses, sedges, and lilies, imperfect chloroplasts produce stripes of green and white tissue. Finally, some leaf variegations are caused by disease, particularly virus infections. Examples are the mottles or mosaics on leaves caused in dandelions by dandelion yellow mosaic and in cabbage by cabbage black ringspot viruses. In some cases the veins on leaves are beautifully highlighted as the chlorophyll is cleared from around the vein cells. Arabis mosaic virus causes this in elder and lettuce big vein virus has the same effect on lettuces. Plants infected in this way are sometimes collected and propagated by man as novelties.

By now it will be clear that a great many of the garden plants whose colours and form we tend to assume are gifts of nature are, in fact, the result of man's interference. They can justifiably be called artificial flowers. It is perhaps debatable whether plants need 'improving' at all and purists may find the very thought of the 're-finement' of nature offensive. However, there is no doubt that work on new ornamental varieties continues at a great pace, and that many people continue to pay large sums for new varieties of garden flowers. For example several years ago a company in the United States of America offered a $10,000 reward to the grower who could successfully cultivate a white marigold (*Calendula*

species). Single specimens of new orchid varieties can cost well over $100 each.

The gardener's use and appreciation of plant colour has run parallel with the art of his time, while cottage gardening, a glorious hugger-mugger of colourful plants can be compared with primitive painting. The Tudors used heraldic-coloured flowers in formal knot gardens. The Stuarts favoured evergreens, including the variegated forms, often using topiary. These in turn led to baroque, architectural pattern-making in parterres with plants used as blocks of colour, a fashion now declined into the beds of annuals in public parks.

Planting as an art form using flower and foliage colour that consciously echoed Impressionist painting was introduced by Gertrude Jekyll (1843-1932) herself a painter. She mixed shrubs with plants and is said to have invented the herbaceous border. By her books and work she taught gardeners to plant sophisticated colour schemes and, in woodland gardens to make use of exotic shrubs like rhododendrons azaleas and ornamental trees, grouped for effect both in summer and autumn.

In today's smaller gardens great emphasis is laid on balance, proportion and outline. Lawns being impracti-cal in small areas, brick, wood and paving often set off plant colour and vice versa. Japanese gardening, with its pure lines, asymmetric forms and delicate colour has had a strong influence. Some exciting work is also being done in different parts of the world using abstract shapes and strong colour contrasts comparable with abstract painting. When planting today, attention is given not only to flower and foliage colour used in harmonies and contrasts but to the shape and texture of each plant and all its parts. Upright or fastigiate shapes are set against low, horizontal or rounded ones, large leaves and flowers near small ones, glossy against matt and light against dark.

With the present feeling for conservation of the environment and with knowledge of the reasons for plant colour and its relationship with animals, plants can be grown that attract butterflies, bees and other insects and also those that offer shelter and food to birds and other wild life.

Whether we prefer wild or cultivated plants, the simple or the elaborate, it is pleasing to know that man's total dependence on plants can be linked with a real enjoyment and appreciation of their intricacies and beauty.

Centre left: A spring garden scene with trees and shrubs grouped in a woodland setting. A dark, fastigiate conifer contrasts with the white cherry tree behind and with the low, rounded and horizontal shapes of pink azaleas, hebes and forget-me-nots in the foreground.

Below left: Colourful plants used in half-hardy summer bedding. Multicoloured leaves of coleus hybrids and scarlet *Iresine herbstii* contrast with the maroon foliage of castor oil plant, *Ricinus gibsonii* and a variegated corn, *Zea japonica variegata*. The under-planting is of silver-leaved senecio, centaurea and helichrysum.

Right: A herbaceous border of the kind designed by Gertrude Jekyll (1843-1932). Plants are grouped according to their shape, height, colour and time of flowering. They include tall delphiniums, rudbeckias, echinops and verbascum with heleniums, salvias, sedums and plants with white flowers and silver foliage.

Glossary

ANTHER Pollen sac producing **pollen**.

ARIL Soft, fleshy outgrowth surrounding seed, which helps to attract animal dispersers.

BATESIAN MIMICRY Type of **mimicry** when one organism copies another to gain a one-sided advantage.

BIOLUMINESCENCE Giving off of light by living organisms such as seaweed, fungi etc.

BRACT Modified leaf associated with a flower, often brightly or contrastingly coloured.

CAROTENOID Type of **pigment** found in cell **protoplasm**, producing a range of yellow, orange, red and brown colours.

CARPEL Leaf-like structure that encloses the **ovule**; sometimes fused together into **ovaries**.

CHLOROPHYLL Green **pigment** found in all green plants, essential for **photosynthesis**.

CHLOROPLAST Small body in plant cell where **chlorophyll** is found and **photosynthesis** takes place.

COMPOSITE FLOWER Flower head or **inflorescence** made up of many **florets** crowded together to look like one flower; a member of the family Compositae.

COROLLA Collective name for petals on a flower.

CORONA Specialized petal-like appendage between **corolla** and **stamens**, e.g. trumpet of daffodil.

CORTEX Outer part of a plant stem or root.

ECHO-LOCATION Way of finding where an object is by bouncing sound 'echo' off it. Used by bats to fly accurately in dim light.

EPIDERMIS Outermost layer of cells of leaf. Also of young stems and roots.

FAMILY Group of animals or plants subdivided into **genera**.

FLORET Small flower growing with several others, e.g. on **composite** flower head.

FLOWER Reproductive structure of angiosperm or flowering plant.

FRUIT Structure containing the plant's seeds, developed from **ovary** and sometimes from other parts of the flower as well.

GENUS (pl. genera) Group of plants or animals, subdivision of **family** and in turn divided into related **species**.

HEMI-PARASITE A partial **parasite**, gaining some of its food through **photosynthesis**, some from another plant.

HYBRID Plant (or animal) resulting from a cross between two different **species** or **varieties**—occasionally between different **genera**.

INFLORESCENCE Group of flowers growing together on special axes, e.g. a spike.

LEGUME Member of pea or bean family Leguminosae.

MIMICRY Here, the way in which plants copy one another or animals in either shape or colour to gain an advantage for **pollination**, seed dispersal etc.

MÜLLERIAN MIMICRY Type of mimicry where plants copy one another and both copied and copier gain an advantage.

MUTATION Change that occurs in a gene and can be inherited.

MYCORRHIZA An association between a fungus and other plants (e.g. flowering plant root). Both benefit.

NECTAR A sugary liquid produced by flowers to attract pollinators.

NECTARY The structure that produces **nectar**, usually in association with a flower.

OVARY 'Female' part of a flower, consisting of fused **carpels**.

OVULE 'Female' reproductive organ containing the egg cell.

PARASITE Here, a plant which does not photosynthesize but lives off another plant.

PERIANTH Collective name for petals and sepals.

PETIOLE Stalk of leaf.

PHLOEM System by which food manufactured in the leaves is distributed throughout a plant.

PHOTOSYNTHESIS The process by which green plants use the energy of sunlight to convert water and carbon dioxide to sugars. Oxygen is produced as a by-product.

PIGMENT Chemical substance which reflects and absorbs light of different wavelengths to produce colour.

PLASTID Small body in cell **protoplasm** where food is manufactured; contains **pigments**.

POLLEN The special **spores** liberated from 'male' reproductive organs in seed plants.

POLLINATION Transfer of pollen from male to female parts of plants.

PROTOPLASM The living tissue of a plant.

SAPROPHYTE Plant that lives off dead remains of plants and animals and does not usually photosynthesize.

SEED Structure by which flowering plants reproduce. Formed after fertilization from the **ovule**.

SPADIX Spike of crowded flowers on a thick fleshy axis, usually surrounded by a **spathe**.

SPATHE Large modified **bract** surrounding and often enclosing an **inflorescence**.

SPECIES Distinct group of plants or animals which can interbreed and produce fertile offspring; a subdivision of **genus**.

SPORE Reproductive cell produced without sexual fusion. Usually liberated in vast numbers from fungi, mosses, ferns etc.

STAMEN Flower structure containing the **anthers**.

STOMA (pl. stomata) Opening, usually on the underside of a leaf, through which gases enter and leave the plant.

VACUOLE Part of cell, containing cell sap.

VARIEGATION In leaves, patterning of colour or of green and white.

VARIETY Plant slightly different from others of same species, perhaps in colour or size only.

VASCULAR BUNDLE Strand of tissue containing the **xylem** and **phloem** systems.

VISIBLE SPECTRUM Range of wavelengths producing colour visible to animals, insects etc.

XYLEM System in which water and minerals travel through a plant from the roots.

Bibliography

Bjorn, L O: *Light and Life*. Hodder and Stoughton, Sevenoaks, 1976

Corner, E J H: *The Life of Plants*. Weidenfeld and Nicolson, London, 1964

Darlington, C D: *Chromosome Botany and the Origins of Cultivated Plants*. George Allen and Unwin, London, 1973

Everard, B and Morley, B D: *Wild Flowers of the World*. Octopus Books, London, 1974

Grant, K A and V: *Hummingbirds and their Flowers*. Columbia University Press, New York and London, 1968

Jaeger, P: *The Wonderful Life of Flowers*. Harrap, London, 1961

Fogden, M P L and P M: *Animals and their Colours*. Peter Lowe, London and Crown, New York, 1974

Frisch, K von: *Bees, their Vision, Chemical Senses and Language*. Cornell University Press, Ithaca, 1950

Gilbert, L E and Raven, P H (eds): *Coevolution of Animals and Plants*. University of Texas Press, Austin and London, 1975

Gorer, R: *The Development of Garden Flowers*. Eyre and Spottiswood, London, 1970

Hvass, E: *Plants that Feed and Serve us*. Blandford Press, London, 1973

Kerner von Marilaun, A: *The Natural History of Plants*. Blackie, London, 1902

McQuown, F R: *Plant Breeding for Gardeners*. Collingridge, London, 1963

Milne, L and Milne, M: *Living Plants of the World*. Nelson, London, 1967

Percival, M S: *Floral Biology*. Pergamon Press, Oxford, 1965

Pijl, L van der: *Principle of Dispersal in Higher Plants*. Springer-Verlag, New York, 1969

Pijl, L van der and Dodson, C H: *Orchid Flowers: their pollination and evolution*. University of Miami Press, Florida, 1966

Proctor, M C F and Yeo, P: *The Pollination of Flowers*. Collins, London, 1973

Ramsbottom, J: *Mushrooms and Toadstools*. Collins, London, 1953

Raven, P H and Curtis, H: *The Biology of Plants*. Worth, New York, 1970

Wickler, W: *Mimicry in Plants and Animals*. Weidenfeld and Nicolson, London, 1968

List of species

The common names of plants vary greatly from place to place. This list gives the latin names for those plants mentioned in the text by their common names alone. Where several species are involved, the abbreviation *spp.* is used.

Alfalfa *Medicago sativa*
Aluminium plant *Pilea cadieri*
Akee *Blighia sapida*
Apple *Maltus sylvatus*
Artichoke, globe *Cynara scolymus*
Arum lily *Zantedeschia aethiopica*
Arum, water *Calla palustris*
Ash *Fraxinus excelsior*
Aspen *Populus tremula*
Avens, mountain *Dryas octopetala*
Avens, wood *Geum urbanum*
Azalea *Loiseleuria procumbens*

Baobab *Adansonia digitata*
Beech *Fagus sylvatica*
Beech, copper *Fagus sylvatica 'purpurea'*
Beetroot *Beta vulgaris*
Bindweed *Convolvulus* spp.
Bird of Paradise flower *Strelitzia* spp.
Bird's eye *Myosotis* spp.
Blackberry *Rubus fruticosus*
Blackcurrant *Ribes* spp.

Bluebell *Endymion nonscriptus*
Borage *Borago officinalis*
Bottlebrush *Callistemon* spp.
Bracken *Pteridium aquilinum*
Broom *Cytisus, Genista* and *Sarothamnus* spp.
Broomrape *Orobanche* spp.
Bugle *Ajuga reptans*
Bullock bush *Templetonia retusa*
Burdock *Arctium* spp.
Burning bush *Euonymus atropurpuratus*
Buttercup *Ranunculus* spp.
Buttercup, Alpine *Ranunculus alpestris*
Butterfly bush *Buddleja davidii*

Calabash tree *Crescentia cujete*
Calla, S. African pink *Zantedeschia rehmannii*
Campion, red *Silene dioica*
Campion, white *Silene alba*
Cardinal flower *Lobelia cardinalis*
Carrion flower, giant *Stapelia nobilis*
Carrot *Daucus carota*
Cashew *Anarcardium occideritale*
Castor oil plant *Ricinus communis*
Catchfly, night-scented *Silene noctiflora*
Catchfly, Nottingham *Silene nutans*
Catchfly, red German *Lychnis viscaria*
Celandine, greater *Chelidonium majus*
Celandine, lesser *Ranunculus ficaria*

Century plant *Agave palmeri*
Chamomile, common *Chamaemelum nobile*
Chamomile, wild *Matricaria recutita*
Charlock *Sinapsis arvensis*
Cherry, sweet *Prunus avium*
Christmas rose *Helleborus niger*
Cinquefoil, creeping *Potentilla reptans*
Cleaver *Galium aparine*
Clover *Trifolium* spp.
Clover, Alsike *Trifolium hybridum*
Cocoa *Theobrana cacao*
Coconut *Cocos nucifera*
Columbine, red *Aquilegia elegantula*
Coltsfoot *Tussilago farfara*
Coneflower *Rudbeckia bicolor*
Cornflower *Centaurea cyanus*
Cotton *Gossypium* spp.
Cowslip *Primula veris*
Cuckoo pint *Arum maculatum*
Cucumber, squirting *Ecballium elaterium*

Daffodil *Narcissus poeticus*
Daisy *Bellis perennis*
Daisy, everlasting *Helychrysum* spp.
Dandelion *Taraxacum officinale*
Devil's hair *Clematis* spp.
Dodder *Cuscuta* spp.
Dogwood *Cornus sanguinea*

Durian *Durio zibethinus*

Ebony *Diospyros* spp.
Edelweiss *Leontopodium alpinum*
Elder *Sambucus nigra*
Elm *Ulmus* spp.
Eyebright, slender *Euphrasia micranthra*

Fig *Ficus* spp.
Figwort *Sarothamnus nodosa, Scrophularia aquatica* and *Scrophularia nodosa*
Flamingo flower *Anthurium scherzerianum*
Flax *Linum usitatissimum*
Fly agaric *Amanita muscaria*
Forget-me-not *Myosotis* spp.
Foxglove *Digitalis purpurea*
Fritillary *Fritillaria melleagris*

Gentian *Gentiana* spp.
Geranium *Pelargonium*
Ginger *Costus speciosus*
Gloxinia *Sinningia speciosa*
Gold of pleasure *Camelina sativa*
Golden rod *Solidago* spp.
Gorse *Ulex* spp.
Granadilla, giant *Passiflora quadrangularis*
Granadilla, purple *Passiflora edulis*
Grape *Vitis vinifera*
Grass of Parnassus *Parnassia palustris*
Grass, sea *Zostera* spp.
Groundsel *Senecio vulgaris*
Gum *Eucalyptus* spp.
Gum, scarlet flowering *Eucalyptus ficifolia*

Hawkweed *Hieracium* spp.
Hawthorn *Crataegus monogyna*
Hazel *Corylus avellana*
Heartsease *Viola tricolor*
Heather *Callum vulgaris, Erica* spp.
Helleborine, broad-leaved *Epipactis purpurata*
Helleborine, orchid *Epipactis helleborine*
Hemp *Cannabis sativa*
Herb paris *Paris quadrifolia*
Herb robert *Geranium robertianum*
Hogweed, giant *Heracleum sphondylium*
Honewort *Trinia glauca*
Honeysuckle *Lonicera* spp.
Hyacinth *Hyacinthus* spp.

Ice plant *Mesembryantheumum crystallifolium*
Indiarubber plant *Ficus elastica*
Indigo *Indigofera tinctoria*
Ivy *Hedera helix*
Ivy, violet *Cobaea scandens*

Juniper *Juniperus communis*

Kangaroo-paw *Anigozanthus* spp.

Laburnum *Laburnum anagyroides*
Laurel, spotted *Aucuba japonica*
Lettuce *Lactuca sativa*
Lily *Liliaceae*
Lily, giant water *Victoria amazonica*

Lily, gloriosa *Gloriosa superba*
Lily, water *Nymphea* spp.
Litmus lichen *Roccela tinctoria*
Loosestrife, purple *Lythrum salicaria*
Lungwort see Spotted dog
Lupin *Lupinus* spp.
Lychee *Nephelium litchi*

Madder *Rubia tinctorum*
Maidenhair tree *Gingko biloba*
Maize *Zea mays*
Mallow, African *Malvaceae family*
Maltese cross *Lychnis chalcedonica*
Maple *Acer* spp.
Marigold *Calendula* spp.
Marigold, marsh *Caltha palustris*
Mayweed *Tripleurospermum inodorum*
Milkweed *Asclepias* spp.
Mint *Mentha* spp.
Mistletoe *Loranthaceae*
Moondaisy, Alpine *Chrysanthemum alpinum*
Morning glory *Ipomoea caerulae*
Mulberry *Morus* spp.
Myrtle *Myrtaceae*

Nasturtium *Tropaeolum majus*
Nightshade, deadly *Atropa belladonna*
Nightshade, enchanter's *Circaea lutetiana*
Nutmeg *Myristica fragrans*

Oak *Quercus* spp.
Oat *Avena sativa*
Old man's beard *Clematis* spp.
Orange *Citrus sinensis*
Orchids:
    bee and fly *Ophrys* spp.
    bird's nest *Neottia nidus-avis*
    butterfly *Platanthera chlorantha*
    common British *Dactylorhiza* spp.
    coral root *Corallorhiza trifida*
    early purple *Orchis mascula*
    fragrant *Gymnadenia conopsea*
    pyramidal *Anacamptis pyramidalis*
    slipper *Paphiopedilum* spp.
    tongue *Cryptostylis leptochila*
Organpipe cactus *Lemaireocereus thurberi*

Paeony *Paeonia obovata*
Pansy *Viola* spp.
Passion flower *Passiflora* spp.
Peacock flower *Moraea villosa*
Pear *Pyrus communis*
Pea, cultivated *Pisum sativum*
Pea, Sturt's desert *Clianthus formosus*
Pelican flower *Aristolochia grandiflora*
Pimpernel, scarlet *Anagallis arrensis*
Pineapple *Ananas comosus*
Pink *Dianthus* spp.
Pitcher plant *Cephalotus, Darlingtonia, Nepenthes* and *Sarracenia* spp.
Plum *Prunus domestica*
Poinsettia *Euphorbia pulcherrima*
Policeman's helmet *Impatiens glandulifera*
Pondweed, broad-leaved *Potamogeton natans*

Poppy, corn *Papaver rhoeas*
Primrose *Primula vulgaris*
Primrose, evening *Oenothera erythrosepala*
Privet *Ligustrum* spp.

Queen of the night *Selenicereus grandiflorus*

Radish *Raphanus sativus*
Raspberry *Rubus idaeus*
Red-hot poker *Kniphofia*
Robin's eye *Myosotis* spp.
Rose *Rosa* spp.
Rose, guelder *Viburnum opulus*
Rowan *Sorbus aucuparia*
Rupture wort *Herniaria ciliolata*
Rust fungi *Puccinia graminis*
Rye *Secale cereale*

St. John's wort *Hypericum* spp.
Sausage tree *Kigelia pinnata*
Saxifrage, golden *Chrysoplenium oppositifolium*
Scarlet sage *Salvia splendens*
Sensitive plant *Mimosa pudica*
Silversword *Argyroxiphium sandwicense*
Snapdragon *Antirhinum majus*
Snowberry *Symphoricarpos rivularis*
Soya bean *Glycine soja*
Speedwell, germander *Veronica chamaedrys*
Spinach *Beta vulgaris cicla*
Spindle tree *Euonymus europaeus*
Spleenwort, common *Asplenium trichomanes*
Spotted dog *Pulmonaria officianalis*
Stinkhorn fungus *Phallus impudicus*
Stone plant *Lithops* spp.
Strawberry *Fragaria* spp.
Sugarbeet *Beta vulgaris erassa*
Sugar cane *Saccharum officinarum*
Sundew *Drosera* spp.
Sweet pea *Lathyrus odoratus*
Sycamore *Acer pseudoplatanus*

Tansy *Tanacetum vulgare*
Teasel *Dipsacus fullonum*
Thistle *Cirsium* spp.
Thrift *Armeria maritima*
Tobacco *Nicotiana tabacum*
Tomato *Lycopersicon esculentum*
Traveller's tree *Ravenala madagascariensis*
Truffle *Tuber aestivum*
Tulip *Tulipa* spp.
Tumbleweed *Amaranthus* spp.

Venus flytrap *Dionaea muscipula*
Violet, dog *Viola canina*
Viper's bugloss *Echium vulgare*

Wallflower *Cheiranthus* spp.
Weld *Reseda luteola*
Wheat *Triticum aestivum*
Willow, goat *Salix caprea*
Willowherb *Epilobium* spp.

Yarrow, white *Achillea millefolium*
Yew *Taxus baccata*
Yucca *Yucca aloifolia*

Index

Acknowledgements

Artists
John Barber: p. 97
Bruce Collins: p. 18
Will Giles: pp. 14, 24, 32, 39, 40-1, 59, 88-9, 104, 107
Diagram Group: pp. 15, 20, 34-5
Lesley MacKinnon: pp. 15, 44-5, 80-1
Charles Raymond: jacket and title page illustration
Michael Woods: pp. 84-5

Photographers
A-Z Photographic Collection: pp. 28, 51, 60, 78, 108, 109
Aquila Photos: pp. 29, 36, 45, 62
Heather Angel: pp. 10, 17, 21, 22, 25, 33, 35, 36, 38, 47, 49, 53, 54, 66, 82, 83, 86, 87, 88, 94, 95, 98, 105
Neville Coleman: pp. 38, 53, 54, 74, 77
Michael Fogden: pp. 18, 20, 21, 28, 36, 47, 48, 54, 61, 64, 66, 70, 72, 74, 84, 87, 89, 106
Stephen Hilty: p. 86
Ray Kennedy: p. 46
Lennart Norstrom: pp. 9, 18, 23, 26, 87, 101
Natural History Photographic Agency: pp. 39, 53, 58, 63
Oxford Scientific Films: pp. 56, 68, 71, 75, 90, 93, 95
John Proctor: pp. 26, 37, 47, 51, 54, 75, 76, 82, 92, 93, 101, 102, 106
E. S. Ross: pp. 12, 24, 42, 45, 51
Harry Smith Horticultural Collection: pp. 5, 19, 22, 24, 27, 52, 62, 67, 73, 82, 85, 103, 106, 108
Peter Ward: pp. 44, 48, 50, 59, 60, 63, 67, 70, 77, 83, 93, 97
Gunther Ziesler: p. 30
The photograph of the unnamed rose on p. 105 was kindly supplied by Anderson's Rose Nurseries, Aberdeen.
The paragraphs on pp. 108-9 on using colour in the garden, and the captions to the photographs on these pages are by Nancy-Mary Goodall.